Leading the 21st Century Church

Leading the 21st Century Church

James Burn

Pleasant Word
PW A Division of WinePress Group

ISBN 13: 978-1-4141-1518-4
ISBN 10: 1-4141-1518-0
Library of Congress Catalog Card Number: 2009906470

To Kingfisher church, for all the amazing leaders
you continue to develop, and to my wife, Jan,
my greatest encouragement.

Contents

Introduction

HOUSTON, WE'VE HAD a problem!" These famous words alerted Mission Control in Houston, Texas, on April 13, 1970, that the Apollo 13 mission to the moon was not going as planned. An explosion, caused by an electrical fault in an oxygen tank, turned a mission of exploration into a rescue mission to bring the astronauts back alive. That successful rescue mission turned out to be one of NASA's finest hours. Those words uttered by Commander Jim Lovell (often misquoted as "Houston, we have a problem"), signaled the start of a rescue plan that brought out the very best in people, both at Mission Control and on the stricken spacecraft.

Sudden crises often do that. Petty problems and issues are put aside in the face of a common enemy or an unforeseen catastrophe. The attack on the World Trade Center in New York City on September 11, 2001, drew a nation together in grief, mourning, and anger. The London bombings on July 7, 2005, produced a similar response in the United Kingdom.

Other crises, however, are slower to build up and are therefore less noticeable. These crises have been with us for so long that they don't galvanize us into action; they don't produce the heroic responses we see in the crises mentioned above. These are crises we've become used to living with, and we largely no longer see them as such—they are just part of "the way things are."

Leadership in the local church is one such crisis. While we find many fine leaders in local churches, the church in general is not producing leaders who are setting the pace for the secular world to follow.

Much has been written on the subject of leadership. Indeed, the twentieth and early twenty-first centuries have seen a dramatic development of the theory and practice of leadership. From the "Great Man" theories of the early 1900s, whereby leadership was understood as an ability one was born with, through the group theory of the 1930s, the trait theory of the 1940s and 1950s, the behavior theory of the 1950s and 1960s, the business-oriented focus of the 1980s to the popularization of emotional intelligence as a key to understanding leadership, the focus on leadership in the past 100 years has developed greatly. However, as Burns rightly notes, "Leadership is one of the most observed and least understood phenomena on earth."[1] This fact is evident by the fast-changing theories on what constitutes great leadership. The arena of understanding and observing leadership has largely shifted from the military to business, with popular writers such as John Maxwell who in his many books (particularly *The 21 Irrefutable Laws of Leadership*) encourages Christian leaders to learn leadership lessons from the secular business world.

While I would contend that we may learn many valuable lessons from secular leadership theory and practice, I believe that there is currently a scarcity of spiritual leaders in the United Kingdom setting the secular leadership agenda. The great Christian social reformers of the late eighteenth and early nineteenth centuries, known collectively as the Clapham Sect, included Wilberforce, who campaigned tirelessly for the abolition of slavery; and Shaftsbury, who among other things campaigned to limit factory working hours for children and adults. These are examples of Christian leaders who brought great benefits to society in general. In contrast, ex-Prime Minister Tony Blair reportedly complained that "he has been unable to follow the example of US politicians, such as President George W. Bush, in being open about his faith because people in Britain regarded religion with suspicion."[2]

Many do not generally consult the church for insights on how to lead well. The church has largely vacated a position of leadership in society, particularly in the United Kingdom. This is one feature of a society that Murray (among others) calls "post-Christendom." He defines this term as follows: "Post-Christendom is the culture that emerges as the Christian faith loses coherence within a society that has been definitively shaped by the Christian story and as the institutions that have been developed to express Christian convictions decline in influence."[3] I believe that an important aspect of this loss of coherence is the decline of leadership, which is felt most keenly at the local church level.

How can we address this problem? How can the church once again not only be well-led but also regain its position of leadership within society? Is this revival even possible? I believe it is. Particularly in times of great uncertainty and insecurity, as experienced in the global financial crisis of the early 21st century, I believe that the church must reemerge to provide moral and spiritual leadership. The world at its worst needs the church at its best!

A large credibility gap, however, stands between the church as it currently is and the church the world would look to for leadership. As Kouzes and Possner rightly point out, "Credibility is about how leaders earn the trust and confidence of their constituents."[4] Where do we start in terms of addressing that credibility gap? How can the church put its house in order? The answer, I believe, lies in developing a workable strategy for identifying, training, commissioning, and releasing new leaders at the local church level. This strategy includes leaders who actually possess the spiritual gift of leadership and actually receive the equipment they need to grow in that gifting. It includes leaders who are mentored well and are encouraged to grow through those "defining moments" when the temptation is to give up or settle for compromise or when there is no obvious or easy "right" path to tread.

Literally thousands of books have been written about leadership, and hundreds relate to church leadership. Therefore, why should you bother with this book? What can one more book possibly add to the already immense pile? I suggest that this book may be especially useful for two reasons:

First, this book is written by someone who is actually pastoring a local church. I have attended many conferences, and I have read so many books that sound good in theory, but don't translate well into real life. I have seen so many leadership tools and ideas that we pastors are invited to "bolt on" to our existing structures in the hope that they will provide surefire solutions to deeply entrenched problems. I have grown tired of books telling me how to lead that are written by people who are not actually leading a local church themselves. Perhaps you have too.

Second, everything I suggest in this book comes from personal experience. I have tried lots of things that don't work and discarded them. In this book I've included some things that *do* work.

At Kingfisher, the network of churches I pastor, we have been on this journey of growing leaders for some years now. We have raised up many leaders and released them into leadership roles as we have sought to narrow the credibility gap. We embarked on this journey because we sensed the Holy Spirit saying, "Houston, we've had a problem!" Do you sense that, too? Then welcome to the journey!

Section 1

The Need to Develop a Leadership Culture

. . . .

Chapter 1

Leadership Culture
in the Local church

THE STRATEGIC DEVELOPMENT OF LEADERS IN THE LOCAL CHURCH

HOW ARE LEADERS appointed in your church? If you are one of those leaders, how were *you* appointed? If your experience was typical of the majority of churches, chances are that a ministry needed leading and that you were judged to be the best person to fill that vacancy. Or maybe you are among a small core of people—generally estimated at 20 percent—who do at least 80 percent of the work in your church. Therefore, when the need arose, you as usual found yourself filling the gap. This common scenario in the majority of churches leads to several issues.

A Need Does Not Constitute a Calling

Just because a need exists—and just because you have the capacity or desire to meet that need—does not mean that God is calling you to lead in that area. Neither does the application of guilt mean that God is calling *you*. Perhaps you've heard something like this: "The children's ministry has no one to lead it. Can you imagine the disappointment on those little faces, not to mention the rejection and lack of worth that will be sown into them if *someone* doesn't step up and run the Sunday school?" It would take a particularly hard-hearted person to withstand that guilt trip for too long. Of course, someone must perform the basic functions of the church, but the question is, are *you* the one God has called to enable that important function to happen?

The apostles of the first church in Jerusalem hit the nail on the head when they realized that they had allowed a need to define their priorities—in this case the need to organize and administrate the food distribution program. Was this distribution program a legitimate need? Absolutely! Was it their calling? Absolutely not! Yet leaders recognize the courage it took to say, "We apostles should spend our time teaching the Word of God, not running a food program" (Acts 6:2). It took courage because if they didn't perform the task, would anyone else step up and take on the food program? And if no one else did, the food program would not have happened. Then people would have gotten angry and started leaving the church! This common fear among leaders encourages many to meet the needs rather than to be free to pursue their God-given calling.

I made this mistake early in my ministry. Kingfisher Church, which my wife, Jan, and I launched in 1993, was in existence for only a couple of years when it grew to about fifty people. When we were meeting at a local school, I would arrive an hour and a half before the service to get the boiler started; it was too old to operate on anything as sophisticated as a timer. After wrestling with this ancient piece of equipment, I would put out the chairs, set up the tables for tea and coffee, and do whatever else that was needed for the church to function. Volunteerism was at fairly low ebb in those days.

I clearly remember one Sunday in particular. After performing these tasks, I launched into the service and realized that the person who was on the rotation to serve tea and coffee had not shown up. I was fuming! I'd just gone ten rounds with the boiler, the place was cold, I was exhausted and fed up with having to do everything myself, and now to cap it all off no one was even available to make the tea and coffee!

I fumed my way through the service. At the end, my voice dripping with sarcasm, I said, "Well, thank you for coming! Having set the building up, led the service, and delivered the sermon, I shall now serve you tea and coffee, as no one else seems to be willing to do it!"

I marched to the back of the hall and loudly turned the kettle on, all the while expecting at least someone to repent in dust and ashes because of his or her selfish, unreasonable behavior.

My sarcasm was completely wasted; people came for their tea and coffee like normal with barely a thank you. I sometimes wonder why I bother with sarcasm.

Later, as I was packing up, someone said to me, "You know, if you wanted someone to step in and do the tea and coffee, you only had to ask!" Not my finest hour.

A Need Is Not a Sufficient Basis for Establishing a Ministry

"Find a need and fill it" is a fine sentiment, but needs are all around us. Proverbs 17:24 points out, "An intelligent person aims at wise action, but a fool starts off in many directions" (Today's English Version). A much more important question looms beyond "Can we do this?" That question is "*Should* we do this?" An important addition to this question is "Should we do this *now*?"

Kingfisher Church has a thriving youth ministry that is involved in some wonderful initiatives, such as a youth café, a music workshop ministry, a creative arts ministry, and much more. But for many years we had no youth ministry even though teens were coming to the church. Parents would say things like, "It's not that we want to leave the church, but the church down the road has got a wonderful youth ministry."

Every pastoral bone in my body wanted to say, "Don't leave! We'll have a youth ministry by next week!" But the reason we didn't have a youth ministry at that time was because God had not raised up the right person to lead that ministry. Either God had made a mistake and taken His eye off the ball, or He was saying that we needed to focus on other priorities at that stage.

We chose to believe that the Lord knew what He was doing. We could trust Him and wait until He raised up the right person to lead this ministry, which He did in due course. Did we lose people as a result of this decision? Yes—and more than a few. However, our fundamental belief about church is that each local church and each individual Christian needs to be "God shaped." In other words, everyone and every church need to bear the shape God has intended for them at this point in time. We should not be shaped by the things God may desire for another day or by people's expectations.

In terms of the local church, we can determine this shaping by asking the question "Who has God sent us?" If God had wanted us to start a youth ministry at that time, He would have sent us a gifted youth leader who also sensed God's calling. Because God hadn't sent someone at that stage, we surmised that the time to launch a youth ministry had not arrived. We chose to trust God.

Even though people were leaving the church to find a youth ministry, God would grow Kingfisher Church as He saw fit and add a youth ministry at just the right time. It was a costly stand, but one that proved to be abundant in God's blessings. Looking back over the years, we now rejoice in a vibrant youth ministry with a gifted youth leader and many teens coming to know Christ as their Lord and Savior. A need does not constitute a calling, nor is it sufficient basis for establishing a ministry.

Appointing Leaders on a Need Basis Leads to a Reactive Approach to Leadership

What does this mean? It means that as far as finding and appointing leaders is concerned, the church is always playing "catch up." We are constantly responding to a present need, which means there is no way to take the time to properly identify potential leaders; to allow them to mature as they are trained, coached, and apprenticed; or to take a more proactive view of where the Holy Spirit is leading the church. We cannot wait until there is a need to start wondering whom we could possibly appoint as a leader to fill the gap. We must be more proactive than that. We must develop a structure for training and developing leaders without being pressured to appoint them to a leadership position before they are ready.

I know about this pressure personally. I became a Christian in 1981 at a David Watson[5] event in the Royal Albert Hall in London, England.. At the time, I was living in a Christian-run hostel in Waterloo, London. Now a Christian, I was eager to join the Bible study group, which was meeting at the hostel and being led by my roommate. I attended the group with great enthusiasm. I was hungry to learn and knew nothing about the Bible, about how to live as a Christian, or about how to pray. The Christian life was all new to me, and I had a lot to learn.

Six months after I became a Christian, my roommate announced that he was moving out. This, of course, meant that the group would need a new leader. I think he adopted the approach of "Who seems the most enthusiastic?" By this, of course, he meant me. The fact that I was so enthusiastic because I didn't know anything didn't seem to register with him. He appointed me, but I was too naïve to realize that I should have turned him down. So now I, who knew next to nothing, was leading a Bible study group of twenty-five people and answerable to no one other than the God I had met only six months before. What could possibly go wrong?

My first challenge was to decide which book of the Bible we should study. I took advice from the church I had begun attending. "Well, as long as you don't dive headfirst into the book of Revelation," someone told me, "you'll be fine!"

The book of Revelation? That sounded interesting. And if *I* was interested, surely everyone else would be too. So, armed with a commentary that seemed unnecessarily complicated, I launched into what would surely be a stimulating Bible study series.

By week two I had open revolt on my hands. Group members had their own deeply entrenched ideas that didn't coincide with what my commentary said. Suddenly, a cohesive, friendly, even placid group was in an uproar, and everyone was irritated wth everyone else. Worse, everyone was irritated with me!

With my tail tucked between my legs, I asked for help from one or two others who had been Christians a lot longer than I. They advised me in no uncertain terms to abandon the path I had embarked on and to head for the book of Acts instead.

This was a wise piece of advice, and I'm so glad I took it. Peace was restored, the group began to pull together, and I realized that if you want to learn to swim, jumping into the middle of the Atlantic Ocean isn't the best way to go about it! Of course, if I had been part of a structure that developed new leaders, I would have realized that fact long before I'd received the chance to unleash my naïveté on those I was trying to lead. I would also have experienced a more structured, less improvised procedure for getting feedback and wisdom.

Far too many local church leaders today, the product of a similar lack of nurture and development, are passing on their experiences to the next generation of leaders. They are waiting for a pressing need to begin looking for who should step into the breach, then plugging them in with no training and only minimal preparation. Such a methodology only sets them up for failure.

THE DEVELOPMENT OF A LEADERSHIP CULTURE

At the local church level, we must radically overhaul our approach to leadership development. In short, we need to develop a leadership culture in the local church. At its simplest, a leadership culture is an environment whereby leaders are recognized, developed, supported, and released. Forman, Jones, and Miller observe, "It is no secret that one of the biggest needs in the church today—all around the world—is well-equipped leadership."[6] They identify the source of this shortfall as follows: "Most churches are strapped for good leadership and have no intentional strategy for developing leaders."[7] Forman, Jones, and Miller advocate an approach they term "church-based leadership development."[8]

Establishing of a leadership culture in the church is not just putting on a training course for new leaders. It places leadership development at the heart of the church. As John Kotter puts it,

"Institutionalizing a leadership-centered culture is the ultimate act of leadership."[9] But while this philosophy may sit comfortably in the secular, business world, is there really any place for such language in the local church? Dan Kimball, a leading figure in the Emerging Church, proposes a helpful bridge between the two worlds, a concept he calls the "Nouwen-Maxwell sandwich."

> How do we lead yet keep our hearts soft? We need to approach leadership with author Henri Nouwen's heart of being like Jesus, compassionately caring for people, desperately dependent on the Spirit. At the same time, if your church grows, you need to develop the leadership skills of casting vision, developing multileveled teams and recruiting and training leaders, like author John Maxwell is well known for.[10]

But for some, the term *leadership culture* conjures visions of the church becoming led by ego-driven, power-hungry people, with the thrust of the church focused on the development of the few who have the spiritual gift of leadership. Would this emphasis not weaken rather than strengthen the church? As such, should it not lead us to conclude that leadership culture is something we should avoid in the local church? After all, Jesus commanded His followers to "go and make disciples of all nations" (Matt. 28:19). Shouldn't the church be in the business of developing a discipleship culture?

Of course, discipleship is precisely what the church should be about. But without developing strong, godly leaders, that discipleship culture will not grow or thrive. Rather than fostering a dependence on the few, a truly healthy leadership culture will ensure that leadership in its various styles is encouraged at every level of the church. As a result, mature disciples will be raised up. Bill Hybels says, "Much is hanging in the balance. It's my conviction that the crisis of mediocrity and stagnation in today's churches is fundamentally a crisis of leadership."[11] Hybels has it right—the health of the church depends on the health of its leadership.

I believe that a leadership culture can and should thrive at the heart of the local church as long as it is developed with the goal of honoring God and implemented with prayer and sensitivity. Indeed, the church is perhaps the ideal organization for a leadership culture to flourish, founded and headed as it is by the ultimate Leader, Jesus Christ Himself.

What Is a Leadership Culture?

Every church—indeed, every organization—has a culture of some sort. Edgar Schein describes *culture* as

> a pattern of shared basic assumptions that was learned by a group as it solved its problems of external adaptation and internal integration, that has worked well enough to be considered valid and, therefore, to be taught to new members as the correct way to perceive, think, and feel in relation to those problems.[12]

Culture, therefore, develops out of a history of shared experiences. As such, no one can impose it, though the leader initiates and encourages it. Culture is only really established when the wider group shares deeply embedded, unconscious assumptions. Until such time as those assumptions and values become unconsciously shared, what passes for culture is, in fact, mere compliance. The leaders, by means of their strong personalities, say how things are going to be, and the group goes along with that. If leaders have only built compliance, the majority of what they implemented dissolves when they move on, and often the culture reverts to how things were before they came.

How can we tell the difference between a genuine culture and mere compliance? We can tell by the gap between the stated mission and the values of a church and by what actually happens. For example, part of the stated church mission may be that "this church exists to spread the gospel among those who don't yet know Jesus Christ." The church may have conducted a sermon series on this theme, study groups, prayer meetings, and so on. But the real questions are these: How many church people regularly share their faith with non-Christians? How much of the church budget is dedicated to specific evangelistic projects? How many church activities are specifically geared toward non-Christians compared to activities for those who are already believers? The real culture of the church is found, not in stated aims and objectives, but in real, underlying assumptions and therefore practices of church members.

The church's stated mission may well be to reach out evangelistically with the life-transforming message of Jesus Christ. But if the underlying assumption about the community is one of fear mixed with feelings of disconnectedness, regardless of how many posters remind us of the mission statement or how many sermons we hear, little committed, joyful evangelism will take place.

So many church leaders have reached the point of despair over this issue. They have faithfully preached, modeled, encouraged, and even passionately implored their congregations to embrace the way forward, only to sense a mixture of apathy and compliance instead of true commitment. They have not truly understood the basic, underlying assumptions of those within the church and addressed those first before trying to change the culture.

Specifically, what is often the case in an organization that is open to change is what Schein calls a "learning gene." This is the shared assumption that learning is a good thing worth investing in and that "learning to learn" is itself a skill to be mastered.[13] If leaders want to see changes in the culture of their churches, their fundamental task is to address this issue and seek creative ways to develop this learning gene in the church. Unless leaders truly understand the culture in which they lead, that culture will prove resistant to their leadership and ultimately cause great frustration and discouragement.

Like every organization, each church has a culture—healthy or unhealthy. To change an unhealthy culture into a healthy one—which, by the way, is a core leadership role—we must honestly answer the question "What really is the culture of our church?"

If an organization's culture refers to the shared, basic assumptions of a group, then leadership culture is the basic, shared assumption that the church needs gifted, mature, servant-hearted leaders who are being raised up in every area of the church and in an accountable environment in order to encourage and enable the development of fully devoted disciples of Jesus Christ. A coherent leadership culture that is beneficial to the local church must incorporate the values of developing strong, Christlike character as well as recognizing and developing the spiritual gift of leadership. This pursuit must take place within a structure that enables its development as a normal part of the life blood of the church, rather than as something separate or added to all other church activities. In short, leadership culture in the local church emphasizes the priority of leadership development as a major expression of the church's life, whether the leader influences one or many.

THE DIVERSE NATURE OF THE GIFT OF LEADERSHIP

David said to the Lord, "Thank you for making me so wonderfully complex! Your workmanship is marvelous—how well I know it" (Ps. 139:14). A unique and wonderfully creative God has designed us to be uniquely and wonderfully made. Therefore, it is no surprise that when He dispenses the gift of leadership, His goal is not to make "monochrome" leaders, all of whom exercise the gift of leadership with the same personality and in the same way. This gift has a wonderfully rich and diverse flavor. A true leadership culture will celebrate this flavor and ensure that diversity is encouraged. This is an important core value for a leadership culture; without it, the danger is that one particular style of leadership will be exalted or normalized. This style may be that of the overall leader, the leadership team, the denomination, or the training institution.

Herein lies a potential weakness of in-house leadership development. Highlighting mentoring as being of particular importance to developing church-based leadership, Forman, Jones, and Miller say that "local church mentors must be spotters of potential."[14] That is absolutely right. For this responsibility to lie solely with the pastor or leadership team would mean that they will overlook many potential leaders. This problem will only grow worse as the church grows and the central leadership team fails to know everyone well.

While Forman, Jones and Miller talk about spotting those who are "exhibiting leadership traits,"[15] we must ask this question: if the mentor initiates the spotting of leadership potential, is not someone's leadership potential discerned through that mentor's "leadership lens"? Consequently, this method could potentially introduce the risk of "like spotting like," which produces rather monochrome leadership as a result. To avoid this problem, we need a more objective way to recognize leadership potential. Goleman, Boyatzis, and McKee identify the following leadership styles: visionary, coaching, affiliative, democratic, pace-setting, and commanding [16] Considering those styles as examples, one can appreciate that a potential mentor who has a more dominant "affiliative" style—that is, a leader who seeks to create harmony by connecting people to each other—would perhaps struggle to effectively mentor someone who has a commanding or coercive leadership approach. To address this problem, Forman, Jones, and Millar cite Fred Smith's checklist of "10 Signs of Potential."[17]

At Kingfisher, we have formulated our own approach to help answer the question "What does leadership potential look like?" There is, of course, no exact science to answer this question. Although one can fill in various assessment forms to evaluate spiritual gifts, including the gift of leadership, one can only really assess whether someone does or doesn't have this gift over a period of time and in a variety of settings. To be a "spotter of potential," as Forman, Jones, and Miller put it, takes time and a deepening relationship. One must also initially sense a spark of leadership giftedness in someone. To that end, we must ask various questions to reveal that potential:

- Are these people influencers? That is to say, when they have an idea, do others listen and give that idea consideration?
- Do they look for new ways to do something, or do they subscribe to the "If it ain't broke, don't fix it" mentality?
- Do those who know them think well of them? Leaders are unhappy to settle for what is safe. They are often challenging to know because they are "change agents," and

change is not an easy concept for many. Those possessing the potential gift of leadership will be respected by those around them.

- Are they dissatisfied with the status quo? Leaders are visionaries; they are able to see what could be and prefer that to what currently is.
- Do they display a commitment to see things through? Many find reasons why their dreams cannot come to pass, but some possessing the gift of leadership are committed to turning dreams to reality. They are willing to persevere and overcome obstacles.
- Are they willing to serve? Do they mind who gets the credit?

The gift of leadership is also affected by one's "spiritual pathway," which Ortberg defines as "the way we most naturally sense God's presence and experience spiritual growth."[18] Though not writing in the specific context of leadership, Ortberg describes seven such pathways—intellectual, relational, serving, worship, activist, contemplative, and creation. A lack of appreciation for one's preferred spiritual pathway will, I believe, have implications for a mentor who is assessing someone's potential gift of leadership. Kotter is right when he notes, "One way to develop leadership is to create challenging opportunities for young employees."[19] However, the assessment of how young employees respond to those challenging opportunities—or "defining moments," as I call them—is rather more complex than many often allow. Perhaps such an assessment should focus more on the character development of the would-be leader rather than on specific responses.

Chapter 2

How to develop leaders in a Local Church setting

THE DEFINING MOMENTS OF LEADERSHIP

ONE CANNOT DEVELOP character in the classroom or learn it from a book. Character is developed in the crucible of challenging experiences, at the crossroads of confusing priorities, and whenever the temptation to compromise arises. I call these character-forming times "defining moments." Even a cursory glance at the Bible reveals that God used defining moments to develop disciples in general and leaders in particular. We can view these defining moments as pain barriers all leaders must confront and break through in order to develop maturity. Our role model in this endeavor is Jesus Himself. In Matthew 14:1–36, Jesus experienced a series of defining moments that would honestly flatten most leaders.

The Defining Moment of Personal Grief

In this passage, Jesus just heard that His second cousin, John, had been put to death in a particularly grisly manner. It's always a shock when someone we know dies. But when a family member has met a tragic end, especially in the type of circumstances surrounding John's death, the impact of that death hits us like a thunderbolt.

The Defining Moment of a Lack of Personal Space

Verse 13 reveals that Jesus needed to get away from others to process His grief and sense of loss and to give His emotions time to heal. Time alone is important for leaders, yet hard to achieve. As Jesus headed off to a remote area, the crowds got wind of where He was going and converged on Him there.

The Defining Moment of Compassion Fatigue

When you want to be alone to recharge or to process heavy things that have happened, it's easy to resent the constant demands and needs of others. When a ringing telephone (even if you don't answer it) invades your first evening home in ages; when the Holy Spirit touches your heart during a time of worship but someone taps you on the shoulder and wants a word; when three people are trying to talk to you at once; when the same person is covering the same ground, making the same mistakes, and not moving on despite the hours you spent with him or her. . . then you as a leader are in danger of developing compassion fatigue. Though Jesus tried to get alone and find personal space, vast crowds wanting His attention confronted Him. The fact that verse 14 records that Jesus "had compassion on them" at that point is remarkable.

The Defining Moment of Feeling Constantly Responsible for People

Verse 23 reveals that Jesus finally found some time alone. He'd dealt with the crowd and sent His disciples off in a boat. Now He spent some quality time alone with His Father. Looking at the lake, however, He noticed that His disciples were in trouble. Once again, He abandoned His need to grieve alone so He could rescue them.

The Defining Moment of Being Assaulted by All Those Demands at Once

All those defining moments occurred in a short period with no recovery period between them. After rescuing His disciples, Jesus was thrust back into the next round of ministry (vv. 34–36). Each defining moment tested Him, but so many coming at once, one on top of the other, must have stretched Him to the limit.

When do we experience defining moments? We experience them during the storms of life. When a storm hits some people, the most pressing question is "Why doesn't God take this storm away or get me out of it?" When He doesn't, we start to lose confidence in God and in the power of prayer. We begin to doubt whether God is real and cares about us at all. We get angry about the unfairness of it all. *After all we've done for God*, we think, *how could He let this happen to us?* This is a natural response to the storms of life. We've all been there, whether the storm was a passing inconvenience or a life-changing, earth-shattering tragedy.

Certainly, the lives of the Christians Peter wrote to had been turned upside down. They had gone from being ordinary, everyday citizens to refugees, often in fear for their lives. All they had done was to choose to trust in Jesus Christ for their salvation. How could God have allowed all this bad stuff to happen as a result? We can essentially boil Peter's answer down to this: God is not the author of random crises. He does not allow His children to suffer for no purpose.

So what *is* God's purpose in allowing storms to hit? "These have come so that your faith—of greater worth than gold, which perishes even though refined by fire—may be proved genuine and may result in praise, glory and honor when Jesus Christ is revealed" (1 Pet. 1:7 NIV). God allows storms because those provide the setting for our faith to be refined. No storm is pleasant. God doesn't like storms, and He certainly doesn't want us to struggle through them. Having experienced various storms in my own life, I'm certainly not seeking to minimize the anguish storms cause. But God doesn't allow storms because He is unable to stop them or is indifferent to them. He allows them because they serve the purpose of being a refining fire. Only during storms do we encounter our defining moments. Faith grows as the result of our growing through a whole series of defining moment experiences.

You will not encounter a defining moment experience in green pastures or beside still waters. Those are the places where God *restores* our souls, not where he *refines* our souls. Our souls need both refining and restoring if they are going to reach maturity, which is God's overriding purpose for our lives. *Our* overriding purpose in life is to avoid the storms—that's only natural—but *God's* overriding purpose is to allow the storms because they provide the most fertile setting for defining moments.

What is a defining moment? A defining moment is a crossroads in our lives. It's a point where everything in me wants to take the easy option, yet deep within me I know that God is calling me to take another path. Maybe things have become difficult for me at church, and I'm finding that life is tough going. What I'd rather do is try another church. Maybe that would be more exciting; maybe they'd sing a different set of songs; maybe what I need is a change. In reality, perhaps God is allowing this dry period in my life to bring me to the point of greater maturity. It may be a different church, but it will be the same God. Maybe God is calling me to stay put, to confront the issues in my life, to deal with them in a godly way, and to move into a more mature relationship with Him—one that doesn't depend so much on external factors.

You will never reach that defining moment without the storm of feeling dry and dissatisfied. Satan's greatest deception is that we are passive victims within that storm, that we have no choice about what we can do. That's a lie! The truth is that as sons and daughters of the living God, we have the power and authority to choose what we believe and how we will react regardless of the storm we are facing. That is the clear message of the Gospels. For example, one day the disciples found themselves in a fierce storm on the Sea of Galilee. "The disciples went and woke him up, shouting, 'Master, Master, we're going to drown!' When Jesus woke up, he rebuked the wind and the raging waves. Suddenly the storm stopped and all was calm. Then he asked them, 'Where is your faith?'" (Luke 8:24–25).

Do you see yourself as a passive victim in your storm? Do you not yet have the faith to realize that you can choose your response to the storm? The obvious but immature response is to command the storm to go away. The more mature response is to identify the defining moment within the storm before taking authority over the storm and commanding it to go away. Don't overlook the defining moment that is always somewhere in the storm.

On another occasion a crowd of thousands traveled to a remote place to hear Jesus speak. Time passed, and the panicked disciples urged Jesus to send the people away to find food. Jesus didn't end that storm prematurely, but said to the disciples, "You feed them" (Luke 9:13). He helped the disciples see the defining moment in the storm.

Don't view the storm as the work of Satan or as evidence that God doesn't care about you without first looking for the defining moment. Peter says, "In this you greatly rejoice, though now for a little while you may have had to suffer grief in all kinds of trials" (1 Pet. 1:6 NIV). It's not grief that causes you to greatly rejoice—of course not. It's managing not to collapse in the face of grief. It's managing not to give in and run away, but rather to rise and face the defining moment, realizing that "having done all…[you *can*] stand" (Eph. 6:13 KJV).

Broadly speaking, we can group defining moments into three categories. Leaders-in-training needs to be guided through all three if they are to grow in maturity and character. The first category is the discovery and development of our identity in Christ. This is the defining moment of self-leadership.

Self-leadership is of crucial importance in leadership development. An inability to lead oneself or the lack of appreciation for the importance of this area severely limits a person's effectiveness in leading others. A specific benefit of self-leadership is that it enables true accountability, which is essential for the emergence of a healthy leadership culture. Accountability only truly emerges in an environment of self-leadership because it requires a commitment to honesty, openness, and integrity. In my leadership experience, both at Kingfisher Church over the past sixteen years and before that in a secular setting, we cannot impose these attributes on others; they must be personal, inner core values nurtured through self-leadership.

The development of self-leadership is fundamental to acquiring the ability to lead others. Self-leadership, however, is not about our defining who we are, but about our discovering whom God has created us to be. While this foundational need to understand our identity in Christ is relevant to all Christians, it is particularly so in terms of meeting the challenge of leadership. Many have made various attempts to address this issue, one notable example being author Neil Anderson. In answer to the question "Who am I?", he compiled a comprehensive list of Bible verses. When put together, the verses create helpful insight into one's identity in Christ.[20] He supplemented this list with a further list, called "Since I am in Christ, by the grace of God . . ." This list details thirty-one different aspects of what Christ has done for us.[21] He concludes, "The truth about who you are in Christ makes such a big difference in your success at handling the challenges and conflicts of life. It is imperative to your growth and maturity that you believe God's truth about who you are."[22] One question in the context of developing a leadership culture in the local church is this: how can we best understand our identity in Christ?

At the most basic level, God has called all Christians to practice the spiritual disciplines of private and corporate prayer, Bible study, fellowship, and Christian service. Building on these basics, Forman, Jones, and Miller suggest three contexts in which church-based leadership development occurs: courses, community, and mentoring.[23] I suggest that we best develop the defining moment of understanding and growing in one's identity in Christ through these contexts. The truths we need to learn about our identity in Christ best lend themselves to the learning environment of a course. As Cloud and Townsend assert, however, "Biblical growth is designed to include other people as God's instruments. To be truly biblical and effective, the growth process must include the body of Christ. Without the body, the process is neither totally biblical nor orthodox."[24]

While Jesus' approach to developing leaders included frequent opportunities for His followers to reach a deeper understanding of their new identity, this understanding was usually taught, demonstrated, and developed in the context of community (for example, Matt. 5:1–16; Mark 9:35; Luke 22:22–30). The third category—that of mentoring—is perhaps the most powerful of all when we apply it to the context of understanding one's identity in Christ. It allows the emerging leader to observe and evaluate the impact that a healthy identity in Christ has on the life and ministry of a leader. Cloud and Townsend see mentoring as best suited to the environment of the local church.

> Mentoring, in our opinion, however, is best done within the context of the "church" for two reasons. First, it makes the character issues, which drastically affect a person's work life, grist for the mill, and, second, it helps to integrate a person's life by eliminating the all-too-common split between work and spiritual life. It is a good thing for a person to be mentored by someone who can see what is happening in his or her overall walk of faith and growth in Christ.[25]

In the context of general spiritual development, Forman, Jones, and Miller say that mentoring involves "bringing all people to maturity in Jesus Christ (Ephesians 4:13)."[26] They focus specifically on "a particular aspect of mentoring in the local church, namely, the training of potential, emerging and existing leaders."[27] While coaching does not presuppose direct experience in the area the new leader is emerging into, mentoring does presuppose such direct, personal experience. This suggests that while coaching would most naturally take place in a more formal setting, mentoring by definition can be both formal and informal, individual and small-group based. The goal of the spiritual mentor is to encourage Christlike character rather than to indoctrinate people into the ways of the organization.

The second broad category of defining moments is best summed up in the question "Who are we?" If the first category of defining moments deals with *self-leadership*, the second category is about *group leadership*. Within this category of defining moments, the leader-in-training is encouraged to ask questions such as "How do I influence people to humbly evaluate whom God has created us to be and therefore what God is calling us to do and then in obedience to Him move forward in the appropriate way?" A spiritual leader is not free to take what is merely the most pragmatic route; a spiritual leader is answerable to God for the decisions he or she makes. This accountability seems to lend weight to Blackaby and Blackaby's definition of spiritual leadership as "moving people on to God's agenda."[28]

Enabling a new leader to understand "Who has God created us to be?" in relation to the group he or she is learning to lead is the necessary precursor to moving those people on to that agenda. Max DePree maintains that "the first responsibility of a leader is to define reality."[29] This statement, however, leaves the leader's task open to misunderstanding. While one interpretation of DePree's statement could well be that a leader's role is to be the source of reality, another—in my view, correct—interpretation is that a leader's first responsibility is to *clarify* reality for those who are following so they will follow God's agenda rather than anyone else's. Nevertheless, despite this ambiguity, DePree's statement has merit since the group's identity must deal with reality rather than self-deception.

The third broad category of defining moments lies in the context of how the group interacts with the overall church. Leaders-in-training need to grow in their understanding of how their particular area of ministry impacts, enhances, and affects the overall church, even if they themselves are not being called into overall church leadership. No area of ministry can be developed in isolation from other areas of ministry, and often the needs and priorities of these various areas of ministry can seem to be in conflict. Defining moments occur at those points of conflict, and those conflicts are often most clearly evident in the area of budgeting.

At Kingfisher, the leader of each ministry area is responsible for his or her own budget. Each year, the leaders are invited to bid for a budget for the following year, and that budget is split into three broad areas: money we need to fulfill any legal or contractual obligations (such as music licenses, insurance, and so on), money we need to continue our existing level of ministry, and money we need for the ministry to expand. The budget holder is required to itemize and justify each area of proposed expenditure. The budget request is then submitted to the trustees for prayerful consideration.

This is a real defining moment for the trustees; they need to hear what God is saying in terms of which overall direction He wants the church to go. They need to discern which budget areas have priority over other areas, in which order new areas of expansion need to be implemented, and how to best communicate the outcome of that process to the budget holders so they and their area of ministry continue to feel valued. It is a defining moment for each individual budget holder as well since he or she is called to see and value not only the needs of his or her own area of ministry but also the overall needs of the church.

Of crucial importance in the development of a leadership culture is a focus on defining moments that lead to an emerging leader's understanding of his or her identity in Christ, of the identity and purpose of the group he or she is currently leading, and of the purpose and identity of the local church in which that group is located. I believe it is important for emerging local church leaders to be exposed to defining moments and encouraged to grow through them because "people judge by outward appearance, but the Lord looks at the heart" (1 Sam. 16:7). The development of the inner life is of crucial importance if we are to develop leaders who are approved by God.

THE ROLE OF EMOTIONAL INTELLIGENCE IN THE DEVELOPMENT OF A LOCAL CHURCH LEADERSHIP CULTURE

The term *emotional intelligence* is a relatively new one. Though it seemingly first appeared in the German publication *Praxis der Kinderpsychologie und Kinderpsychiatrie* in an article by Leuner in 1966 [30] and subsequently as the title of an article by Peter Salovey and John Meyer in 1990, one could argue that the study it points to is not new at all. Plato, after all, wrote that "all learning has an emotional base." Describing emotional intelligence as a form of social intelligence, Salovey and Meyer point to the ability to understand one's own emotions and others' emotions and to use this information in how one handles oneself in social interactions. Salovey, Mayer, and Caruso developed a framework for understanding emotional intelligence as representing an intelligent system for handling emotional information. This framework consists of four branches: emotional perception/identification, emotional facilitation of thought, emotional understanding, and emotional management.

Key to their article is the contention that emotional quotient (EQ) (taken here to mean the measure of a person's emotional intelligence) can be scientifically tested via a performance-based tool, the Multifactor Emotional Intelligence Scale (MEIS), later revised to become the Mayer, Salovey, and Caruso Emotional Intelligence Test (MSCEIT). Salovey, Meyer, and Caruso have since refined their definition of "emotional intelligence" to the following: "Emotional Intelligence is the ability to perceive emotions; to access and generate emotions so as to assist thought; to understand emotions and emotional knowledge to reflectively regulate emotions so as to promote emotional and intellectual growth."[31]

Popularized by Daniel Goleman in 1995, the study of emotional intelligence has since grown dramatically. Goleman's book *Emotional Intelligence: Why It Can Matter More Than IQ* contends that our emotions play a far greater role in thought, decision making, and individual success than many previously thought. Focusing on both personal competence and social competence, Goleman proposes a model consisting of five key competencies: self-awareness, self-regulation, motivation, empathy, and social skills. Goleman, both in his coauthored book, *The New Leaders*, and in other articles, focuses particularly on emotional intelligence in the area of leadership. He claims,

> I have found…that the most effective leaders are alike in one crucial way: they all have a high degree of what has come to be known as Emotional Intelligence…my research, along with other recent studies, clearly show that Emotional Intelligence is the *sine qua non* of leadership.[32]

Goleman sees that emotional intelligence makes up 90 percent of the difference between star performers and average performers in senior leadership positions.[33] Such leaders distinguish themselves because they "know their strengths, their limits and their weaknesses."[34] While Goleman and others point to various biological and chemical activities in the brain as a means of understanding emotional intelligence, they claim that it is by no means a purely physiological consideration regarding the growth of emotional intelligence in a leader. There are various structures in the human brain, collectively known as the limbic system, that are involved in emotion, motivation and memory. A person's limbic system can be developed, a fact that is especially important for a leader to understand.

> Quite simply, in any human group, the leader has the maximal power to sway everyone's emotions…Followers also look to the leader for supportive emotional connection—for empathy. All leadership includes this primal dimension for better or worse.[35]

If one took the enthusiasm of Goleman, Boyatzis, and McKee at face value, it would seem that emotional intelligence should play a central role in the development of a leadership culture. However, the key question we must ask is this: does an understanding of emotional intelligence help meet the challenge of developing a leadership culture *in the local church?*

The study of emotional intelligence is a relatively new discipline. As such I would advocate caution in terms of a too-enthusiastic or uncritical adoption of it before one has thoroughly investigated whether it is compatible with the Bible's assertion that leadership is a spiritual gift (see Rom. 12:8). As such, I would challenge Goleman's assertion that "Emotional Intelligence is the *sine qua non* of leadership."[36] To make it so would be to diminish the importance of divine calling and God's prerogative to choose "things the world considers foolish in order to shame those who think they are wise" (1 Cor. 1:27).

Various tests have been devised to test for emotional intelligence and to establish EQ, among the most prominent being those developed by Goleman;[37] Reuven Bar-On;[38] and Meyer, Salovey, and Caruso.[39] Common to these tests is a lack of cultural context that, in my opinion, seriously undermines the usefulness of such testing. Matthews, Zeidner, and Roberts, in reviewing the approach to testing emotional intelligence developed by Meyer, Salovey, and Caruso, suspect a cultural bias to these tests, dictated by the academic experts selected to arrive at the best answers to the test questions.

> There are also doubts about the cultural fairness of expert judgments. Consensus scoring substitutes popular standards for the standards of a few individuals, on the assumption that the pooled response of large normative samples is accurate. However, there seems to be little direct evidence for this supposition, and consensus may be influenced by culture or gender-based stereotypes and by beliefs that are popular but false…Being in step with other people's beliefs may well be advantageous, but it is doubtful it can be labelled a "true intelligence".[40]

This issue of contextualization—of defining the "norm" by which to grade one's EQ—John Edmiston helpfully addressed in his e-book, *Biblical EQ*. He offers the emotional life of Jesus Christ as the model for measuring emotional intelligence. "It's central premise is that Jesus Christ is the model for our emotional life and that the sanctification of our emotions is a work of grace involving the power of the Holy Spirit working in the committed Christian."[41] While this approach would appear to have the advantage of introducing a more objective means of weighing emotional intelligence (in Eph. 4:13, for example, Paul points to the goal of measuring up to the full stature of Christ), one still must ask how objective this approach really is. Surely Jesus Christ, who was both fully God and fully man, was subject to contextualization regarding His humanity. This fact raises the need for a thoughtful understanding of Romans 8:29.

Does being made in the likeness of Christ include the measuring of our emotional intelligence against Christ's? It is my belief that while one should not impose modern, secular emotional intelligence tests on the historical figure of Jesus Christ, Edmiston's point is that Christ exemplifies the key emotional intelligence competencies of self-awareness, self-regulation, motivation, empathy, and social skills. Here, I believe, is where emotional intelligence can make a positive contribution to the challenge of creating a leadership culture in the local church—not in testing and scoring these key competencies, but in providing structured opportunities for reflecting upon them and developing them in the life of each emerging leader.

The challenge of developing a leadership culture has as its fundamental goal the development of leaders who understand and practice leadership with the heart and tenacity of Jesus Christ. To achieve this goal, the subject of emotional intelligence has an important role to play. Specifically for leaders, an insight into and growth in the key emotional intelligence competencies mentioned above will be necessary for the emerging leader to negotiate the defining moments he or she encounters in a healthy leadership culture.

The outcome of growing through these defining moments is the ability to create resonance among a group of people, where *resonance* is defined as "the positive driving of others' emotions."[42] These defining moment experiences help the leader develop a sense of how others in the group are feeling, how the group as a whole is feeling and how best to harness the individual and group emotions to bring maximum growth in the group as well as in the individuals. When this happens in a group, the group experiences a sense of resonance. Goleman, Boyatzis, and McKee assert that for a leader to successfully create resonance, that leader will "act according to one or more of six distinct approaches to leadership and skillfully switch between the various styles depending on the situation."[43] This skillful switching between styles of leadership, they argue, is made possible only as the result of a high degree of personal and social awareness.[44] While such a skill is undoubtedly valuable in creating resonance, I feel that there is a danger of taking this to a chameleon-like extreme, with the leader presenting followers with whatever persona appears to achieve the best results. Sensitivity and flexibility are good leadership traits, but taken too far they can become counterproductive, with followers becoming unsure about the "real identity" of the leader.

In my experience, people trust leaders who have an openness and authenticity about them, more so than leaders who are skilled at saying the right things for the sake of creating resonance. The challenge here is to take the positive of adopting the style of leadership most appropriate to the situation and blending it with an openness and authenticity. That challenge is best met in the context of the leadership culture being argued for in this section, with defining moments being reflected upon and allowed to enable greater personal insight and understanding. Does the study of emotional intelligence enable this journey? I believe that an appreciation of the core competencies of self-awareness, self-regulation, motivation, empathy, and social skills are central to the development, not just of leaders, but of all healthy, balanced disciples. However, they cannot be claimed as new insights in the field of emotional intelligence—they have always been core essentials for healthy leadership development. Furthermore, for the reasons described so far, I do not believe that the challenge of creating a healthy leadership culture in the local church, where the spiritual gift of leadership is being discerned, developed, and released, will be met by the implementation of and reliance upon emotional intelligence tests.

THE PERSONAL GROWTH OF A LEADER

The challenge of creating a local church leadership culture that produces leaders who are able to lead in the twenty-first century centers on not only the teaching of leadership theory but also the development of leadership character, hence the focus on defining moments and emotional intelligence. The development of leadership character is also developed through encouraging the emerging leader to bring theological reflection on past personal experiences. Zaleznik points out,

In *The Varieties of Religious Experience*, William James describes two basic personality types, "once-born" and "twice-born."People of the former personality type are those for whom adjustments to life have been straightforward and whose lives have been more or less a peaceful flow since birth. Twice-borns, on the other hand, have not had an easy time of it. Their lives are marked by a continual struggle to attain some sense of order.[45]

Zaleznik makes the point that "leaders tend to be twice-born personalities, people who feel separate from their environment."[46] The truth of this statement is certainly born out of my own experiences of encountering and learning from setbacks and mistakes and overcoming barriers. In fact, it would seem that the greater the calling, the more challenging the setbacks, mistakes, and barriers. Rather than seeing these as disbarring someone from leadership, we can see them as trials God allowed to grow leadership character in someone. One can also see examples in the Bible—leaders such as Moses (Ex. 2:1–10), who was separated from his mother and his cultural heritage; Joseph, who was rejected by his brothers and sold into slavery (Gen. 37); and David, who was consigned to tending the family flocks of sheep (1 Sam. 16:1–13).

In my experience as a church leader who has developed and trained new leaders over the past sixteen years, I have come to view this "twice-born" element as increasingly important. When assessing potential new leaders, I look more and more to life experiences and evaluate how potential leaders have dealt with and learned from them. I believe that developing "twice-born" leaders is particularly important if the local church is to meet the challenge of being relevant to the world it is trying to reach in the twenty-first century. It enables the church to provide leadership in a "twice-born" world.

I contend that it takes a church led by "twice-born" leaders to speak to any authority in this world. I do not intend that statement to diminish the authority of the message we preach, but rather to highlight the increasing need to establish credibility in order to be heard in a postmodern world. People assess the person before they assess the message—this is every bit as true in the arena of leadership as it is in the arenas of preaching and evangelism.

To be "twice-born" requires more than the presence of difficulties in someone's past. It takes someone who has addressed, understood, and worked through those difficulties. As Blackaby and Blackaby note,

> A significant number of well-known Christian leaders grew up in dysfunctional homes. Many of these leaders have experienced God's healing grace, which has transformed them into healthy, successful leaders. Others, for whatever reason, are unwilling or feel unable to allow God's grace to free them from their troublesome pasts. These people emerge as adults with feelings of inferiority, inadequacy and anger, all despite their outward success.[47]

Can someone who was not "twice-born" aspire to leadership? I believe the answer lies in understanding that "twice-born" does not merely refer to a difficult, challenging past. It refers to how one theologically reflects on this past in terms of understanding theodicy. It requires one to learn from the past and to grow through it, allowing difficult, challenging experiences to mold and build one's character. As such, we cannot grade "twice-born" experiences in the sense that experiences would need to reach some predetermined level of difficulty; each person's "twice-born" experience is unique. The challenge for a healthy leadership culture is to help the emerging leader via the mentoring process and defining moment experiences to identify and reflect on his or her particular "twice-born" experiences, enabling positive character growth and deepening emotional intelligence to emerge.

Chapter 3

Releasing new leaders

THE DEVELOPMENT OF A LEADERSHIP MODEL THAT IDENTIFIES, APPRENTICES, AND COMMISSIONS NEW LEADERS

HOW ARE WE to identify, train, and release such leaders into the life of the local church? For a leadership culture to be more than just a "paper exercise," one must have a strategy leading to the development and implementation of a leadership model. What kind of model, however, would be suitable for a local church? Blackaby and Blackaby note the following:

> The trend towards a CEO model of ministry has changed the churches' evaluation of effective leadership. The pastor's ability is measured in terms of numbers of people, dollars and buildings. The more of each, the more successful the pastor...Christian organizations seem willing to overlook significant character flaws and even moral lapses, as long as their leader continues to produce.[48]

The trend of secular companies to implement leadership models that focus on producing successful results at the expense of character issues is, I believe, a dangerous one for the church to pursue because it focuses the church away from its key calling—to "go and make disciples" (Matt. 28:19). The issue of character development is crucial in the formation and development of local church leaders. Indeed, as Blackaby and Blackaby point out, "If Jesus provides the model for spiritual leadership, then the key is not for leaders to develop visions and to set the direction for their organizations. The key is to obey and to preserve everything the Father reveals to them of his will."[49]

A leadership model—the structuring of leadership development—that meets the leadership challenge faced by the local church must have as its fundamental core value the development of mature disciples of Christ who understand and operate their spiritual gift of leadership in a way that honors God. What might such a model look like? Fundamental to a successful model is the belief that leaders are not grown instantly but over a period of time. That growth comes from three sources—through getting knowledge, through growing in character, and through gaining experience as they put the first two sources into practice. A successful model will provide structures for a leader-in-training to gain knowledge, to grow in character, and to practice what he or she is learning. One major deficiency of local church leadership training is this: Someone perceives a need and appoints someone to meet that need. The result is that the person meeting the need is now viewed as a "leader." This system, however, has failure written all over it, both for the new leader and for the church. New leaders need help to grow and develop through various stages before they are released into full leadership.

The Discernment of a Definite Calling

Thom Rainer observed in his research that "all the breakout leaders whom we researched have a definitive testimony of God's call in their lives for vocational ministry, particularly in the local church."[50] This sense of calling is fundamental to spiritual leadership and involves both an invitation and confirmation from other leaders in the church and an inner sense of calling from God (Acts 1:23–26). How does one assess calling? An effective leadership model will allow and encourage reflection to assess whether one is indeed being called to leadership. It will also give tools to help others with that assessment.

It is important not to underestimate the importance of calling. As Sanders points out, "Spiritual leaders are not elected, appointed, or created by synods or churchly assemblies. God alone makes them."[51] The assessment of that calling—indeed, the assessment of calling to any area of service—should form part of the church's discipleship process. Forman, Jones, and Miller rightly highlight this fact when they say, "To multiply leaders for our church, we must focus first on multiplying mature disciples."[52] The leadership call comes out of a solid base of maturing disciples; therefore, a prerequisite for a functioning leadership model is a discipleship process in which one is encouraged to discover and try out potential spiritual gifts. Just as importantly, he or she should grow in character by being presented with and growing through the defining moments mentioned above.

Forman, Jones, and Miller identify the goal in the leadership development process of producing "servant-leaders who know God, ('head'), exhibit Christlike character ('heart') and are effective in ministry and mission ('hands')."[53] While they limit these categories to the context of leadership development, I would suggest that these categories are equally useful in assessing whether one who has a potential spiritual gift of leadership is, in fact, at the right place to take that gift further. Such an approach highlights the need for opportunities to learn, particularly about the subject of spiritual gifts (specifically the gift of leadership), opportunities to respond to situations in a Christlike manner (with appropriate feedback and reflection), and opportunities to practice that potential gifting. These opportunities should form part of the general discipling process as they were with Jesus and His followers, but specifically in the area of leadership development.

To assess one's potential leadership calling and to have others assess that potential calling, one must have a forum for teaching on the gift of leadership ("head"), a reflection on one's attitude toward those one may potentially lead ("heart"), and a controlled environment in which to begin putting into practice the skills God has imparted ("hands"). That forum is what we at Kingfisher call our Introduction to Leadership course.

In preparation for the Introduction to Leadership course, we encourage existing leaders to identify someone in their groups who potentially displays the beginnings of a gift of leadership. They then invite that person to pray about attending the Introduction to Leadership course. Having agreed to do this and attended the course, that group leader has another conversation with the person in question on the subject of how that person feels regarding a possible call from God to leadership. The leader, in conjunction with the coach and other members of the leadership development team, then prayerfully considers whether the time is right for that person to proceed further into the leadership model. While many specialized areas of leadership exist—for example, children's ministry, music, and small group leadership—the emphasis at this stage of Introduction to Leadership is on the general nature of the spiritual gift of leadership and its core competencies.

The Development of Communication Skills

One obvious leadership need is the ability to communicate. That communication must occur both horizontally (with others) and vertically (with God, both personally and by enabling others in this area). Communication of both types is a complex business because it depends on not only our ability to impart and receive information but also our propensity to filter that information through past and present experiences. As Mackay says, "People are not blank slates on which we write our messages. People are pulsating bundles of attitudes, values, prejudices, experience, feelings, thoughts, sensations and aspirations. They are active, not passive, even when they are listening."[54]

Good communication then requires emotional intelligence, specifically an empathy toward the emotions, feelings, impulses, and drives generated within the limbic systems of those they are leading. As already noted, the limbic system of each person in any given group interacts with the limbic systems of others and primarily with the limbic system of the leader. A leader who is therefore unable to contribute to this mix of emotions and influence it in a positive way will be unable to motivate or envision those he or she seeks to lead.

How does one learn to communicate more effectively? A fundamental step in this process involves understanding the communication process. The organization Mind Tools[55] suggests that the communication process involves the source, the message, the encoding of that message, the channel used to deliver that message, the decoding of the message, the receiver, the feedback, and the context.[56] I would suggest that this is true for both aspects of communication being considered here. Mind Tools authors highlight the need to remove barriers that exist at each stage of the communication process. These barriers include an unclear understanding of why and what one is seeking to communicate, a lack of clarity in the message, a lack of understanding of the recipient's mindset and worldview, a lack of forethought regarding the method of the message's delivery, a failure to appreciate the recipient's ability to decode the message, and a lack of appreciation and understanding of the context and cultural setting within which the message is being sent and received. Communication also breaks down due to a lack of attention to feedback, both verbal and nonverbal. In addition to the barriers highlighted by Mind Tools, I would add differing theological outlooks—even biases—between the source and the receiver. This barrier can lead to a complete breakdown in communication and even anger and animosity.

Understanding and growing in the ability to communicate, both horizontally with others and vertically with God, is a prerequisite of healthy leadership and therefore a necessity we should focus on in the development of a leadership model. We need to engage in a head, heart, and hands approach through formal teaching in terms of understanding the process of the various forms of communication; through personal study, reflection, and growth; and through group exercises that help develop communication skills.

It is instructive at this point to ask, "How did Jesus teach?" An investigation of His teaching methods reveals His use of the head, hands, and heart approach. It is important to note that Jesus employed no one teaching method per se in the sense that the recipients of His teaching shaped the approach He adopted. His audiences varied in size and maturity, from those who followed Him as curious onlookers (John 2:23, to the believing disciples (John 2:11), to the seventy (Luke 10:1), to the twelve (Mark 3:14), and to the inner three (Matt. 17:1–2; Mark 14:33). As Mark 4:33-34 points out, "He used many such stories and illustrations to teach the people [the curious onlookers], as much as they were able to understand. In fact, in his public teaching he taught only with parables, but afterward, when he was alone with his disciples [the believing disciples or perhaps the seventy or the twelve], he explained the meaning to them."[57]

When analyzing Jesus' teaching methods, it is important to note that He placed importance on three areas—content (orthodoxy, relating to head—Matt. 22:29), outworking (*orthopraxis*, relating to hands—Matt. 23:3), and the character of the one teaching (relating to heart—Matt. 10:26). While in a secular environment one could argue that the teacher's moral and spiritual standing does not fundamentally affect his or her interaction with those who are being taught, for those following Jesus' model, this is not so. Likewise, Jesus' injunction to His listeners to "go and do the same" (Luke 10:37) and His sending out of his disciples to practice what He had taught them, bestowing upon them His authority (Luke 10:1–16), links these three elements in Jesus' approach to teaching.

Within this overarching statement, we can see how Jesus developed His approach to teaching, noting that He tailored His teaching method to suit both the occasion and the audience. When appropriate, Jesus taught in such a way that His listeners gained a deeper understanding and knowledge of God (head), using formal teaching opportunities such as the Sermon on the Mount (Matt. 5–7), group discussions (Matt. 20:20–28), and times with individuals (John 21:15–19). He gave opportunities for His disciples to put what they were learning into practice (hands), sending them out with authority to "cast out all demons and to heal all diseases" (Luke 9:1), always giving opportunities for feedback after the event (Luke 10:17–20). He took every available opportunity to develop

Christlike character in His followers (heart), using reflection on events that had impacted them (Matt. 17:14–20), personal demonstrations of humility (John 13:1–17), and direct challenge (John 6:60–69). Thus we can see that the approach to training new leaders I have argued for here would seem to align with the general approach Jesus took.

The Development of an Outward Focus

This stage of leadership "is found in leaders who consistently and persistently move the church to look beyond itself,"[58] says Rainer, citing Peter and John's encounter with a beggar at the temple gate called Beautiful (Acts 3:1–10) as an example. At this level of leadership we can begin to appreciate an emerging difference between the leader and the manager. As Kotter helpfully puts it, "Management is about coping with complexity…Leadership, by contrast, is about coping with change."[59] Following this distinction, Peter and John demonstrated true leadership by identifying the new opportunity that had presented itself, not only for the man they were in a position help, but for the spread of the gospel. They developed this outward focus by encouraging the church to look beyond itself to the needs of the outside world.

How might we develop this level of leadership in the local church as part of a leadership model? One key way is to encourage leaders-in-training to participate in short-term mission opportunities in which they will be exposed to environments different from their own and find opportunities to grow both in their Christian lives and in the area of leadership through acts of service, personal reflection, and growth within community. Having personally led several short-term mission trips both to India and to Malawi, Central Africa, I have observed firsthand the profound impact this kind of opportunity has on team members. Stripped of many home comforts we so often taken for granted and forced to rely on God's provision for both physical and spiritually needs, many have experienced dramatic and sustained character growth and spiritual growth beyond the end of the mission trip.

Many similar opportunities are available closer to home, such as serving homeless people in the area or caring for the elderly. At Kingfisher, we are involved in The Food Bank, a charity that collects food from local churches, schools, and supermarkets and then distributes it to those in need because of domestic abuse, delayed benefits payment, homelessness from drug dependency, or some other reason. The possibilities are endless, but the benefits are great.

The Development of Genuine Passion

This aspect of leadership development is not an assessment of personality, but rather an opportunity to grow in the area of perseverance. Passion is defined here as the will and enthusiasm to continue leading despite adverse, sometimes hostile circumstances. Rainer again cites Peter and John[60] as two examples of passionate leadership (Acts 4:19–21). It is in this area that the potential for discouragement is great, particularly in the area of local church leadership.

The history of Kingfisher Network, which I pastor, bears witness to this. Kingfisher started life as an independent church, launched by just twelve people with no financial backing, no spiritual oversight, and no external support at an emotional level. For the first few years, I received no fixed salary. Raising a young family, this presented my wife, Jan, and me with various financial challenges and many discouragements relating to the growing pains of a local church. The benefits of this situation were that it encouraged me to develop a growing reliance on the Lord and a refining and clarifying of the call to church launching in my life. It caused me to confront the issue of just how committed I was to this venture as one challenge followed another, threatening to overwhelm our small congregation. I see this now as a vital, refining period in my life that enabled crucial growth in me and which laid the groundwork for subsequent growth and the fresh challenges of leading what is now a much more complex and challenging church.

My early experiences led me to the conclusion that both mentoring and coaching are urgently needed at this stage. While mentoring and coaching share certain similarities, there are crucial differences between them. Those differences lead me to the conclusion that both are necessary in the process of leadership development. The coaching and mentoring network defines these terms as follows:

> Mentoring, particularly in its traditional sense, enables an individual to follow in the path of an older and wiser colleague who can pass on knowledge, experience and open doors to otherwise out-of-reach opportunities. Coaching on the other hand is not generally performed on the basis that the coach has direct experience of their client's formal occupational role unless the coaching is specific and skills focused.[61]

An association exists in some people's minds between mentoring and the discredited Shepherding movement of the 1950s through 1970s. However, when mentoring is correctly understood and applied, it is very different. While with shepherding the focus was on authority and covering, upon control and hierarchy, mentoring focuses upon someone who has greater experience serving the apprentice and seeking to impart wisdom for development and growth. Shepherding focuses on control and covering; mentoring focuses on serving, equipping, and releasing. Shepherding ultimately robs people of their God-given freedom of choice, whereas mentoring encourages them to become all that God has created them to be. To continue developing as a passionate leader requires both the development of leadership skills and strategies, and the wisdom that comes from someone who has already encountered the challenging, and discouraging issues the leader-in-training is now encountering.

While the first apostles and founders of the early church did not have the benefit of either coaches or mentors in their pioneering work, they did have the benefit of several years of firsthand instruction from Jesus Christ and a relationship with Him. The Holy Spirit also specifically empowered them for the task of establishing the fledgling church. In addition, they benefited from mutual accountability (Gal. 2:11–16), a leadership insight we would do well to understand and apply today. The church of today has the benefit of two millennia of leadership experience that should also be thoroughly utilized. The leadership model being proposed here must have both the structure required for the more formal discipline of coaching and the more informal mentor relationships to develop. While gaining perspective and support from both a mentor and a coach is a vital part of maintaining passion in leadership, the fundamental role of both needs to be that of encouraging a close, personal relationship with Jesus Christ, as exemplified by Peter and John (Acts 4:13).

The Development of Courage

As stated above, my contention is that "leadership…is about coping with change,"[62] and that change involves "moving people on to God's agenda."[63] Consequently, we can see that leadership involves making and standing by decisions that are often less than popular. This aspect of leadership development—judging which stands to take, what "moral authority"[64] is required, whether the leader has sufficient supply of it, what the cost will be, and whether that cost is worth it—is one that comes predominantly with experience and with the aid of reflection, both personal and with the aid of a mentor. Reflection on personal experience—including an understanding of personal motivations, weaknesses, triumphs, and lessons learned—needs to be an expectation of leadership development. I will focus on this expectation in the section entitled, Authority and Accountability in the Leadership Culture of a Local Church.[65]

However, to grow through personal experience requires a structure that enables the developing leader to be suitably "stretched" without becoming disheartened. Rohnke's comfort, stretch, panic model is a helpful tool to consider at this stage and one we make use of in our leadership development program at Kingfisher Church. Rohnke proposes that each person has three zones: comfort, stretch, and panic. While most of our activities tend to be in the comfort zone, it is in the stretch zone that our challenges to grow lie. Therefore, the stretch zone is where we experience the most fruitful development. One person's "stretch," of course, is another person's "panic," hence the need for the tailoring of individual learning or reflecting experiences at this stage of the leadership model. We can find an example of the development of this leadership aspect in an incident involving Peter in Acts 5 when Peter confronts Ananias and Sapphira. Confrontation, though inevitable in the area of leadership, is often feared and shied away from; thus it is seldom done well. Conflict resolution, however, is an essential tool every potential leader needs to learn. As Tacitus put it, "The desire for safety stands against every great and noble enterprise."[66]

Kingfisher Network has enshrined this commitment to grow in the challenge of conflict resolution in the fourth of our seven core values: "We seek to grow Biblical Community, based on loving kindness, honesty, integrity and a commitment to conflict resolution."[67] It is a skill all emerging leaders need to be encouraged to develop if we are to see the growth of mature churches.

The Development of Legacy

Over the past sixteen years, I have found that far too little attention has been given to the development of legacy. A church in its infancy, such as Kingfisher was, tends to give scant thought to leaving a legacy; the emphasis is more on survival and short-term growth. The major leadership issues during the early years of Kingfisher Church related to coping with the various crises that assaulted us, rather than planning to hand the baton over to the next generation of leaders.[68] A vital part of leadership development, however, must be the value of enabling and encouraging others to minister. This leadership style equates to the distinction that Carl George, building on Lyle Schaller's work, made twelve years earlier between "sheepherder" leaders and "rancher" leaders. While "sheepherding" "makes the pastor available as the primary care giver to everyone who will respond,"[69] "ranching" is about seeing that people get cared for, "which means that you develop and manage a system of care giving that will include as many of your church's lay leaders as possible."[70]

It is my contention that a leadership model that does not have both the ethos of leaders developing next-generation leaders built into it and the tools to enable that development to happen is both deficient and doomed to ultimate failure. The leadership model we will consider in Section Four answers the question "How are next-generation leaders developed?" However, the question still remains: "What structure would best accommodate the assessment of leadership potential in people and allow them to embark on a process of self-assessment?" I would suggest that we best approach the answer by exposing the potential leader to the defining moments analyzed and proposed above ('Who am I?'; 'Who are we?'; 'How do we relate to the church at large?') in a coherent and structured setting, adopting the head, hands, and heart approach. The question arises—"How should such next-generation leaders be exposed to these defining moments?" I propose a training experience of specific length that incorporates the head, hands, and heart approach, exposing leaders-in-training to experiences that enable key the developments we have just considered.

AUTHORITY AND ACCOUNTABILITY IN THE LEADERSHIP CULTURE OF A LOCAL CHURCH

For the local church to experience a healthy, positive leadership culture, however, a healthy understanding of both authority and accountability is key. According to Johnson and VanVonderen, failure in this regard can lead to "spiritual abuse," which is "the mistreatment of a person who is in need of help, support or greater spiritual empowerment, with the result of weakening, undermining or decreasing that person's spiritual empowerment."[71] In distinguishing between strong spiritual leaders and systems, and between abusive spiritual leaders and systems,[72] they draw to our attention just how subtle the differences are. Ronald Enroth maintains that "abusive churches, past and present, are first and foremost characterized by strong, control-oriented leadership. These leaders use guilt, fear, and intimidation to manipulate members and keep them in line."[73]

It is unclear how widespread spiritual abuse is. However, even the possibility of its existence points to the need to clearly define the scope and limits of a leader's authority and to whom and in what manner leaders are accountable. I contend that setting up an accountability structure is easier than enforcing one. I believe that the crucial ingredient to making accountability actually work is the relationship that exists between the various partners in that accountability network. In reality, accountability works on a voluntary basis; it is an informal contract of goodwill that will only be as real as the relationship between the mentor and the emerging leader. An additional issue emerges here—like tends to produce like. Consequently, to ensure the success of real, healthy accountability, which is more than a theoretical exercise, we need to properly address the issue of authority.

To address the question of what authority actually is, we must first ask the question of where it comes from. The *New Bible Dictionary* says, "Such authority as men have is delegated to them by God to whom they must answer for the way they use it."[74] Consequently, legitimate authority exercised by a spiritual leader will possess the character and heart of God. Specifically, Jesus taught that, unlike worldly leaders who "lord it over" others, spiritual leaders should adopt a different attitude: "But among you it will be different. Those who are the greatest among you should take the lowest rank, and the leader should be like a servant" (Luke 22:26). Menno Simons, one of the Mennonite Church founders, has well described this sense of the leader's calling to serve:

> Spiritual authority is never to make the rebel conform; its only purpose is to enable the obedient person to live a holy life. Therefore, it rests on submission and obedience freely given. Furthermore, spiritual authority has only spiritual means at its disposal; its only weapons are prayer, scripture, counsel and the power of a holy life.[75]

Why is the outworking of the authority issue so problematic for the local church? Frost and Hirsch argue that we can trace the immature state of the church to the absence and undervaluing of the fivefold ministry (apostles, prophets, evangelists, pastors, and teachers) described in Ephesians 4:1–16. They argue that while the whole church is called to this fivefold ministry (for brevity's sake, they use the acronym APEPT), the role of the church leadership is to embody such ministry.[76] They contend that the church's failure to recognize and develop these ministries has kept the church from developing as a mission-oriented church[77] in a post-Christendom era.

I agree with this conclusion and would contend that while the roles of prophet, evangelist, pastor, and teacher have received varying degrees of emphasis within the local church, particularly from the latter half of the twentieth century to date, many have largely overlooked the subject of apostleship in particular, to the church's detriment.

Indeed, the existence of modern-day apostles is a contentious issue. Cannistraci cites Vinson Synan as noting, "Most people in church history who have claimed to be new apostles have been branded as heretics and excommunicated from the church."[78] However, Paul's message in Ephesians 4:11–13 seems to be that the gift of apostleship will not die out "until we all come to such unity in our faith and knowledge of God's Son that we will be mature in the Lord, measuring up to the full and complete standard of Christ" (v. 13). Indeed, it would seem that the mature, fully grown church is dependent on the presence and activity of apostles; in fact, in my view, little emphasis on the office of apostle is one reason for the lack of maturity in the church.

Cannistraci, like Frost and Hirsch, sees the whole church as being called to be "apostolic" in the sense that every member is, as in the early church, an "active missionary."[79] However, while the church in general is called to be an "apostolic people" (John 20:21), Cannistraci defines an "apostle" as being "one who is called and sent by Christ to have the spiritual authority, character, gifts and abilities to successfully reach and establish people in kingdom truth and order, especially through founding and overseeing local churches."[80]

In this, Cannistraci differs from Frost and Hirsch, who would rather drop the use of the noun *apostle* in favor of the adjective *apostolic*.[81] I believe that Frost and Hirsch's position is a mistake because it blurs the attributes of authority and scope of the apostle's ministry that Cannistraci helpfully highlights above. Just as all Christians are called to be evangelistic, though not all are called to the office of evangelist, so all are called to be apostolic ("sent") people (John 17:18), though not all are called to the office of apostle (1 Cor. 12:28–30; Eph. 4:11).

This distinction between the office of apostle and the general calling to be an apostolic people enables a clearer understanding of the specific character requirements of those called to this level of ministry. However, as I have said, of the fivefold ministry in general, apostleship in particular is a very contentious one. For the modern church, the major difficulty with the office of apostle comes from the damage done by the Shepherding movement and the notion of "covering," or spiritual oversight. As Frank Viola has put it, "Let us widen the question a bit. What do people really mean when they push the 'covering' question? I submit that what they are really asking is, 'Who controls you?'"[82]

While the Shepherding movement did not start off with the intention of controlling or dominating others—indeed, it found its genesis in the writings of Watchman Nee[83]—it became synonymous with words such as *hierarchy*, *controlling*, and *spiritual abuse*. The architects of the Shepherding movement, the so-called "Fort Lauderdale Five,"[84] were drawn together out of a desire for mutual accountability and support. As this laudable aim spread among other pastors and leaders, so mutual submission and accountability gave way to hierarchy, rules, and power. Although many Christian leaders denounced the Shepherding movement as it grew both in popularity and in its damaging excesses, its influence became international in scope and continued into the 1980s. Various abuses of spiritual authority culminated when the Fort Lauderdale Five officially ended the Shepherding movement in 1986.

The enduring legacy of the Shepherding movement in the context of leadership is a real problem with the issue of authority. In one of this movement's worst excesses, believers were expected to give "absolute, unquestioning submission to their leader."[85] As a reaction, often out of deep hurt and damage, many now reject the notion of spiritual authority. For many, spiritual authority has become tantamount to spiritual abuse. However, as many have often noted, the remedy of abuse is not disuse but proper use.

The tragedy of the Shepherding movement is that though it began out of a desire to bring spiritual depth and growth to disciples of Christ, one fundamental leadership aspect was overlooked: Jesus said, "Whoever wants to be a leader among you must be your servant, and whoever wants to be first among you must become your slave" (Matt. 20:26). The argument about leadership in general and apostleship in particular became one of submission and covering—not submission of the leaders to serve the followers, but submission of the followers to the authority of the leaders. This is the aspect of leadership Jesus was specifically addressing when He said, "But among you it will be different" (Mark 10:43). The greater the call is to leadership, the greater the call is to be a servant. The ultimate example of being a servant, of course, is Jesus Christ, who willingly gave His life on the cross for us.

How ironic it is that the purpose of the fivefold ministry outlined in Ephesians 4 is to bring the body of Christ to maturity, yet this ministry's apostolic aspect has often been handled so immaturely that the opposite effect has occurred.

At Kingfisher, the chairperson of the trustees cleans the men's toilets every week. The senior pastor vacuums the main auditorium at least once a week. The elders regularly serve in other, unglamorous ways—not because we can't find volunteers, but because serving others keeps our hearts attuned to what leading really means.

Service is character forming. This truth reminds us that Jesus Christ took a bowl of water and a towel and washed His disciples' feet. He then told them, the original apostles and future leaders of the church, to go and do likewise. One can be called to be an apostle. But unless one develops servant-hearted character alongside calling, that calling will not translate into truly godly ministry.

Over the period that I have served in the position of developing new leaders, I've noticed a recurring theme: one can teach leadership skills and provide the environment that encourages character to grow, but one cannot teach character. Many who possess identifiable gifts of leadership have been sidelined due to character issues, two of which are a willingness to embrace servant leadership and a freewill commitment to be in accountable relationships. The environment that encourages character to grow will include positive challenges in these two areas in particular. However, the emerging leader's responsibility is to respond to the challenges with reflection, analysis, prayer, and appropriate action.

Intrinsic to the leadership model I am proposing is the testing and growth of character alongside the teaching of leadership skills. The head, heart, and hands approach to each defining moment outlined above lends itself well to the opportunity to develop character. At each level of development within the leadership model, the leader-in-training is accountable to someone who possesses more maturity in his or her leadership gift. This person, in turn, is accountable to someone else for his or her spiritual health and growth. The leader-in-training should be assessed on an ongoing basis in the following areas:

- Does the leader-in-training display an ongoing freshness and growth in the personal spiritual disciplines of prayer, Bible study, personal holiness, and integrity?
- How does the leader-in-training react to setbacks, challenges, and difficult people? Can he or she remain positive and solution oriented? Does he or she maintain personal biblically informed core values under pressure?
- Does the leader-in-training display an openness to accountability and, when necessary, correction? Is he or she able to learn from mistakes?

This ongoing assessment will form the basis of a regular, formal review to be conducted between the leaders-in-training and those to whom they are accountable. This review should not imply that the leaders-in-training must conform to a "corporate image," but rather that they should display ongoing growth in Christlike character within their God-given personality. This information is then shared with the senior church leadership to assist in determining when and whether someone is ready to be recognized as a leader and be thus commissioned.

THE COMMISSIONING OF LEADERS

While pastors, ministers, and leaders within established denominations and various emerging church streams are ordained or commissioned according to the practices of the denomination or organization, this practice often seems to be missing for volunteer leaders in local church-based training. I suggest that this is an unfortunate oversight since the commissioning ceremony achieves several vital objectives:

- It follows the model Jesus gave to the first apostles (Matt. 28:18–20)—a vital aspect of reestablishing Frost and Hirsch's APEPT ministry.
- It signifies a sense of confidence from the church leadership to the leader-in-training, an agreement and solidarity that the person is ready for a leadership role.
- It clarifies the direction the person should take in the outworking of the leadership gift that has been identified and developed. One is "commissioned into" a leadership role.

All of the above is possible only with the development and introduction of a leadership model as the tangible expression of a leadership culture in the local church. Central to the development of character in the leaders-in-training—a vital part of the apprenticeship process—is the role of the mentor, as mentioned above. It is the mentor's role to address these character issues and to recommend when a leader-in-training has completed the apprenticeship process satisfactorily, a judgment that involves more than merely completing the set training courses. It includes the assessment of growth in character at each of the defining moments.

The new leader, now commissioned, then becomes accountable to a more experienced leader, still within the framework of a coaching and mentoring process. Within that framework, the new leader will be guided and encouraged to seek out other potential leaders, beginning the process of helping them assess whether it's the right time for them to embark on the leadership process.

Nurturing apprentice leaders takes time, energy, and a good amount of patience—all three resources Jesus found that He needed to give His disciples when He spent three years training them.

- They followed Him.   Matthew 4:18–20

- They traveled with Him and   Matthew 13:1–23
  learned from Him both privately
  and publicly.

- They were given opportunities   Luke 10:1–16
  to practice.

- They were taught how to cope   Mark 9:14–29
  with success and learn from failure.

- Jesus developed their attitudes   Matthew 20:20–28
  and character.

- He exposed their basic motivation   Matthew 16:22–23
  to them.

- He nurtured them, cared for them,   Luke 22:31–32
  and prayed for them.

Key Aspects of Jesus' Approach to Apprenticeship

If Jesus found it so vital to invest time and energy in apprenticing new leaders, then it is a task all leaders should take seriously. How did Jesus set about apprenticing new leaders? Here are some key aspects:

Jesus' Approach to Apprenticeship Involved a Clear Call

Mark 1:14–20 is an example of how Jesus called two people into the role of apprentice. It involved the following:

- A clear call to commitment ("Come, follow me," v. 17)
- A clear understanding of what the goal of this apprenticeship would be ("I will show you how to fish for people!", v. 17)
- A clear understanding of the scope of the undertaking ("And they left their nets at once and followed him," v. 18)

Jesus' Approach to Apprenticeship Involved Specific Teaching

- Teaching about how to pray (Matt. 6:5–15)
- Teaching about how to minister (Matt. 17:14–21)
- Teaching about the nature of leadership (Matt. 18:1–9)
- Teaching about the heart of God (Matt. 18:10–14)
- Teaching about what to proclaim publicly (Matt. 10)

Jesus' Approach to Apprenticeship Involved Time Spent in Relationship Building

- He recognized the need to spend time relaxing with His disciples (John 2:1–2).
- He knew His disciples individually, not just in terms of what position they held (John 10:27).
- He developed friendships with them (John 15:13–15).

Jesus' Approach to Apprenticeship Involved Providing Opportunities to Minister

- He gave them authority—that is, His own mandate—to minister (Mark 6:7).
- He gave them clear goals and boundaries (Mark 6:8–11).
- He challenged them to attempt great things, but was careful not to place unrealistic burdens of the need to achieve the impossible (Mark 6:11).

- He ensured that they had adequate support (He sent them out two by two—Mark 6:7).

Jesus' Approach to Apprenticeship Involved Feedback

The seventy-two returned full of joy from their mission (Luke 10:17–20).

- Jesus rejoiced with them in their excitement.
- He pointed them beyond their immediate joy to help them see the wider picture.
- He refocused them away from the euphoria of the moment to where their real joy should lie.

Jesus' Approach to Apprenticeship Involved Commissioning

In Matthew 28:16–20, the disciples received the Great Commission.

- The commission clearly gave direction and scope to what Jesus expected of them in the future.
- It gave authority to minister.
- It moved them from one role (that of apprentice) to another (that of minister).

Jesus' Approach to Apprenticeship Involved Ongoing Support, Training, Encouragement, and Feedback

- Jesus promised to be with them "to the end of the age" (Matt. 28:20).
- He promised to ask the Father to give them a Counselor—the Holy Spirit—to always guide them into truth (John 14:16 and John 16:13).
- He continued to guide and give counsel (Acts 1:4-5).

Releasing Apprentice Leaders

Discerning the right time to release an apprentice and give appropriate levels of responsibility is of crucial importance. It is not just a simple matter of determining when the apprentice completes all the modules in the leadership model your local church has adopted. In fact, releasing an apprentice into a full leadership role has far more to do with developing character than with completing modules. Many excellent potential leaders have experienced difficulty and disillusionment because they were given inappropriate levels of responsibility too soon. Conversely, others have been held back when they were ready to be released to do the works God had prepared for them.

Apprentice leaders can feel frustrated because they are impatient for responsibility and desire to take on a full leadership role. They perceive that their mentors are overcautious or even afraid to let them go for fear of being overshadowed or overtaken. Conversely, apprentices can be so in awe of their mentors that they lack confidence that they will ever manage to rise to the standard their mentors set for them.

Pitfalls in the Process of Releasing

- **When mentors are insecure about the gifting of their apprentices**
  King Saul spotted leadership potential in David and took responsibility for mentoring him. However, Saul became jealous of David when people compared them and cast Saul in an unfavorable light.
  "Saul has slain his thousands, and David his tens of thousands" (1 Sam. 18:7 NIV).
  The result: "The next day an evil spirit from God came forcefully upon Saul" (1 Sam. 18:10 NIV). Saul's jealousy made him vulnerable to spiritual attack. (Note: "An evil spirit from God" is a way of saying that all spiritual forces are under God's ultimate control and operate only within divinely determined boundaries.)
- **When a mentor gives too much responsibility too soon**
  Joseph undoubtedly had the spiritual gift of leadership, as Genesis 37–50 records. However, his father failed to encourage Joseph's character to mature, leading to Joseph's

unwise, rash statements about his future leadership role (Genesis 37:5-10). This led to his brothers' negative reaction to him and their decision to get rid of him by selling him into slavery.

- **When an apprentice feels in awe of his or her mentor, leading to a   lack of self-confidence**
  Elijah was a man held in such high esteem that Elisha could not imagine doing without him, let alone stepping into his shoes. "The company of the prophets at Bethel came out to Elisha and asked, 'Do you know that the LORD is going to take your master from you today?' 'Yes I know,' Elisha replied, 'but do not speak of it'" (2 Kings 2:3).
- **When an apprentice feels frustrated by not being given more   responsibility**
  King David's son, Absalom, had a checkered career. He killed his brother, Amnon, for raping their sister, Tamar (2 Sam. 13). This murder led to his flight from Jerusalem. When he returned, David forgave him and received him back (2 Sam. 14). Absalom, however, was impatient to assume authority from his father and plotted to do so by force (2 Sam. 15). Because of his impatience and dishonesty in seeking to grasp something he was not ready for, his life ended in disaster (2 Sam. 18).

A Better Approach

Another approach of releasing an apprentice, as highlighted by Barnabas in the book of Acts, presents us with an instructive model.

- Barnabas went looking for Saul because he recognized Saul's leadership potential (Acts 11:25–26).
- Barnabas took the lead teaching role at Antioch, using his influence to introduce Saul and establish his credibility.
- Barnabas was prepared to share his ministry with Saul, seeing this change as from the Lord rather than as a threat to his status (Acts 12:25–13:3).

- Barnabas allowed Saul to grow increasingly though gradually in stature by having the maturity to step back (Acts 13:6 and following).
- From Acts 13:42 on, the two are referred to as "Paul and Barnabas" rather than their previous designation, "Barnabas and Saul." Barnabas successfully made the transition from being Paul's mentor to being his coworker without feeling sidelined or threatened. He did so by being confident in how God had gifted him and because he was truly a servant of the Lord. He recognized Paul's speaking gift and was content to let that flourish. He was there to offer advice and guidance, but recognized that Paul must increasingly make his own way in life. Therefore, when Barnabas knew Paul was making a mistake about Mark (Acts 15:36–41), he did not pull rank and demand that Paul obey him. Instead he parted company with Paul. Barnabas was later proved right about Mark, who became one of Paul's most trusted friends (2 Tim. 4:11).

SUMMARY

The challenge of developing leadership in an environment where structured authority is viewed with suspicion is best dealt with not by imposing authority on a local church from without but by growing and developing leadership from within. This strategy presupposes the existence of a leadership culture and within that the development of a leadership model that enables the identification, character development, and skills development of potential leaders. Such a leadership culture enables a holistic approach to leadership development through reflection upon defining moments and through the growth of emotional intelligence, as encouraged and overseen by mentors and coaches. Emerging leaders are assessed not only in relation to acquiring skills but also in relation to growing character—all leading to a commissioning event, where mentors recognize and release emerging leaders into full leadership ministry in the local church.

Section 2

The Need to Address the Issue of Trust

Chapter 4

· ·

If you're not trusted, you can't lead

THE LOSS OF LEADERSHIP TRUST AND THE CRITICAL NEED TO
REGAIN IT

T RUST IS A core leadership ingredient. People follow leaders
on the basis of their trust. Consequently, when trust is
broken, leadership is damaged and often destroyed. In a
volunteer-intensive organization such as the local church, the
issue of trust and the development of leadership trustworthiness
are key challenges, particularly at a time when many struggle with
"suspicion of authority. The Bible is open to many interpretations
and is but one of many religious writings."[86]

Putting the Issue in Perspective

Trust is of crucial importance. Without trust an organization
lacks cohesion, which Bennis terms "the emotional glue of all
institutions."[87] Nancy Ortberg affirms this need for trust from her
own experience: "You will never be able to develop teams to their
full potential unless you create an environment of trust *person by
person* in your organization."[88] The issue Ortberg raises is that trust
must be earned at the personal level rather than from a distance.
Leadership is, as Csorba maintains, "character in motion."[89]

Character is assessed, not fleetingly and from a distance, but as the leader becomes accessible and vulnerable at a personal level, such that the leader's character can be observed and assessed. Reynolds reports, "A recent MORI poll found only 15 percent of the British public trust multinational businesses to be honest and fair, while 25 percent trust the newspapers."[90] Clearly we see a crisis of trust in regard to the public perception of leadership. Can the same be said of church leadership?

Opinion polls vary as to how much people trust their church leaders. Focusing on a survey conducted by an Irish newspaper, the *Sunday Tribune*, the National Secular Society reports that "sixty three percent of Catholics say they have lost their trust in the clergy."[91] A poll undertaken by Ipsos MORI, a leading market research company in the UK and Ireland, which was conducted in April 1997 among 997 adults in the United Kingdom, revealed that 71 percent of those polled trust the clergy to tell the truth.[92] A larger 2006 poll of 2,074 people revealed that that figure had increased to 75 percent.[93] These figures may suggest that the perceived need to focus on trust and its development in the context of local church leadership in the United Kingdom is overstated. According to the 2006 Ipsos MORI annual poll undertaken on behalf of the Royal College of Physicians in the UK of trustworthy professions , the level of public trust in clergy is comparable to that of public trust in judges. However, I suggest that this comparison is too simplistic. For a true comparison, the categories in which trust is measured must be identical. People expect spiritual leaders to be trustworthy, not just in their professional lives, but in their private lives as well. It is unclear whether this particular poll set the same standard for other professions.

Trust—A Character Issue or a Leadership Tool?

If the trustworthiness of those in authority, particularly in spiritual authority, is such an issue in these postmodern times (and I'm arguing that it is), then we must ask an important question. How can we address this issue in the local church so leaders can develop in trustworthiness and congregations can find encouragement to trust their leaders? Bennis and Townsend identify various ingredients when developing an environment for addressing this issue of trustworthiness and developing the peoples' trust in their leaders. We may call such an environment a "trusting environment."

Developing such an environment, Bennis and Townsend maintain, requires "congruity, consistency, caring, competence—as well as good listening skills and the ability to promote understanding and empathy throughout an organization"[94] These ingredients reflect the components of emotional intelligence, which we have already discussed, and underline the link between the emotional intelligence of leaders and the trust the congregation invests in them. One may argue that a "trusting environment" is established as a result of the development of self-awareness, social awareness, self-management, and relationship management. Trust begins to grow as resonance is established. Similarly, trust recedes (though compliance may grow) in a dissonant environment.

Should we regard the development of trustworthiness as a character quality or more as a leadership tool? Csorba maintains that "we honor moral leadership, only if it proves handy."[95] This pragmatic approach to trust seems more damaging to the cause of developing leadership than openly acknowledging that trust does not exist and is unneeded. For trust to be real, it must be at the very core of the leader's character—indeed, leadership is built on the character quality of trustworthiness. For that trustworthiness to be merely a device undermines the very contract on which leadership is based.

Reynolds argues for the superiority of the trust-based relationship: "In a relationship of trust, people will do things for you not because they have to (as in the power relationship), not because they hope it will do them good in the end (as in the hope relationship), but because they genuinely want to."[96] He qualifies this statement by acknowledging that it is not always the case that people want to do what needs to be done.[97] Within such a relationship must exist a high degree of accountability and dire consequences for the relationship when trust is broken. To function well, a trust-based relationship needs clearly-defined boundaries and expectations.

The Development of Trust as a Core Value in the Local Church

Whether one takes Bennis and Townsend's core ingredients of trust, as mentioned above, or Reynolds's ingredients of competence, openness, reliability and equity,[98] it is clear that discussing trust in the abstract is insufficient. To develop trust—particularly the trust of leadership—as a core value in the local church requires an analysis of what makes and breaks trust and of the development of a structure within which trust can be nurtured and grown.

Theological Grounding

Similar to Reynolds's ingredient of competence, for a spiritual leader to find trust within the local church context, that leader must possess an adequate grounding in terms of theological study. Trust is earned, and a fundamental element of that is the confidence that is engendered when the would-be leader displays theological competence. Several options are available: attendance at a Bible college, studying at home via a correspondence course, group learning in the local church environment via a locally developed theology course, or a mixture of the above. One positive aspect of the leadership culture I am arguing for—and within that the leadership model a church can develop—is the flexibility of choosing the training method that best suits the occasion. While a leader being developed for a church-wide teaching role may well need the credibility and greater depth of a formal, even accredited course of study, it may well be that a small group Bible study leader would benefit more from an in-house, homegrown course. The presence of a leadership model by no means precludes the option of using external training courses, but rather it allows for a greater freedom to provide the most appropriate training for a leader-in-training at each stage of his or her growth.

However, I would suggest that the use of local church-based training whenever possible—whether course material is home-grown or imported from an external source—offers a number of significant advantages when developing a leadership culture within the local church.

Increased Accountability

Church-based theological training allows for increased accountability in that the very leaders to whom the emerging leaders are eventually going to be accountable are involved in the learning, development, and assessment process throughout the training period. This enables a much greater degree of insight into the strengths and weaknesses of the emerging leader and establishes a healthy accountability relationship prior to the commissioning of the emerging leader. The accountability spoken of here, of course, is internal accountability. The freedom of the leadership model to encourage the emerging leader to embark on an accredited course then opens the way for external accountability. While that is not necessarily an essential component of leadership development, it does provide the benefit of seeing that local church leadership in a helpful, wider context, ensuring compatibility between what is taught at a local level and what is taught at a wider level.

Increased Flexibility

As I noted in the consideration of emotional intelligence, flexibility is needed in the learning experience to maximize the different ways people assimilate information. Obviously, not everyone learns in the same way – different learning styles suit different people. In light of this observation, the development of church-based theological training has the potential to be creatively flexible in terms of the learning process, not least because the local church is setting the curriculum at a local level. This has the potential of allowing the curriculum to be more responsive to individual needs.

Increased Transparency Leading to Increased Trust from the Congregation

Reynolds highlights the superiority of "trust-based relationships" over "power relationships" or "hope-based relationships."[99]

Trust-based relationships are those in which "people will do things for you not because they have to (as in the power relationship), not because they hope it will do them good in the end (as in the hope relationship), but because they genuinely want to."[100] For such a trust-based relationship to develop between emerging leaders and those they will eventually be leading, transparency must exist, not only in the person but in the process. Congregation members need to see the emerging leader engaged in the process of theological learning, reflection, and application. This transparency best takes place in the context of church-based training, particularly as the emerging leader has opportunities to apply theological knowledge in the context and among the people he or she will eventually be leading.

The leader needs to give careful thought not only to the most appropriate styles of learning but also to the content, depth, and breadth of what is taught. One danger, for example, is merely teaching the "party line" that reflects the theological biases of the existing church leadership. Consequently, although advantages exist for a local church to write its own in-house course, we can gain much from exposing students to viewpoints the local church may not agree with by mixing with students from other churches and traditions. A healthy, in-church training program will seek to offer these benefits, though one must admit that exposure to other viewpoints is one of the major benefits when emerging leaders attend an external training course. Agreement is not the fundamental issue; developing the ability to debate and analyze issues calmly and effectively, however, is an important skill for a leader to develop, as is the ability to develop an understanding of issues from other perspectives, even allowing them to inform and challenge one's own position. We need to learn how to walk hand in hand without completely seeing eye to eye!

Chapter 5
Recovering lost trust in leadership

EXPLORING EXPECTATIONS CHRISTIANS HAVE OF THEIR LEADERS

EXPECTATIONS PEOPLE HAVE of their leaders are symptomatic of the context in which we live. Johnston, reflecting on the subject of preaching, notes,

> In a postmodern context, where authority is suspect and people mistrust those in power, what may make the difference as to whether one listens or tunes out is the perceived attitude of the preacher. "Does the speaker care about me?" or "Can I trust what I am about to hear?"[101]

I suggest that those a leader is seeking to lead in the twenty-first century should ask similar questions. Johnston is suggesting the expectation of greater connection, vulnerability, and transparency from those who would seek to preach than was perhaps the case in the past. He goes on to say,

> In connecting with the needs of the listener one should be aware that within postmodernity, the "heart," or intuitive and emotional response evoked within the listener, is oftentimes a more powerful

and fruitful avenue than the "head," which is a more cognitive and rational approach. Addressing the needs of the listener will involve more than taking an intellectual approach to issues. It also means touching the emotional and intuitive areas.[102]

Does this mean that followers are no longer concerned with issues of the head? Put another way, Bosch, who writes in the context of mission, asks the question: "Does this not mean that we have just jumped from the frying pan into the fire, that having (rightly) rejected the myth of objectivity, we have now fallen prey to uncontrolled subjectivism?"[103] This statement would suggest a level of unjustified gullibility in followers. Along with Bosch, who sees a return in the last four decades to "a (modified) realist position in which concepts like truth and rationality are again being upheld,"[104] I believe that many possess a greater awareness of the connectedness between head and heart and that leadership credibility comes as a leader demonstrates that connectedness. That demonstration comes about as the leader demonstrates "humility and self-criticism,"[105] these being two principle ingredients in the development of trustworthiness in a relationship.

Developing a Strategy for Growing Trustworthiness in Those in Leadership Positions

Taking the above into account, how can we develop trustworthiness in those in leadership positions? In light of postmodernism, perhaps now more than ever before potential followers desire to feel connected to those who would lead them. They need to experience that connection at the head, hands, and heart levels, which is achieved through developing Bennis and Townsend's or Reynold's core ingredients as described above. In one sense, to talk about the development of trustworthiness as a strategy is to highlight a major cause of the lack of trust in leadership. As Csorba points out, "Leadership primarily must be a moral endeavor."[106] He maintains that "leadership is character in motion,"[107] this being the outworking of an inner conviction rather than a strategy that would suggest a pragmatic device.

Recovering lost trust in leadership

This is a great point that Csorba makes, but I would add that a leader must be aware of what builds and undermines trust. For a leadership model to be effective, it must provide opportunities for the developing leader to build a track record of trustworthiness and ensure that trust is not unnecessarily jeopardized through easily avoided errors. While learning from one's own mistakes is good, learning from the mistakes of others is even better. As such, I submit that talking about the need for strategy in terms of growing trustworthiness is indeed appropriate. But what is it that increases trustworthiness? Csorba, reflecting on secular society, maintains, "We desperately require a moral leadership, yet dismiss it. This is because we have become a society that places effective leadership over moral leadership."[108]

I believe that we can broadly level this charge at the church as well. Any strategy to grow leadership trustworthiness must primarily focus, not on increased effectiveness, but on the development of good character. C. S. Lewis referred to those lacking character as "men without chests."[109] It must be the goal in any leadership development strategy for the local church to be developing "leaders with chests"—more than merely people who can produce results. How do we develop "leaders with chests"? An environment where trustworthiness in leaders is developed will focus on the following:

ENCOURAGING REFLECTION ON AND ILLUMINATION FROM PAST EXPERIENCES

As noted earlier, Zaleznick's categories of "once-born" and "twice-born" leaders, with the latter having experienced and being deeply affected by life's traumatic experiences, are crucial ones in the area of leadership development. A "twice-born" leader will have not only experienced trauma and struggle in life but also reflected on those experiences and been transformed by them. This is not to diminish the benefit of learning from the experiences of others. However, I would contend that while other people's experiences can inform—inspire even—only our own experiences have the power to transform us at the deepest level of our being. As Cloud and Tonwsend put it, "Through the process of pain, growth happens. I hate it, but it is good."[110] It is the crucible of those experiences, within which we experience God's comfort, that encourages us to reflect and equips us to lead others effectively (2 Cor. 1:4).

THE FORMING OF A TRUSTING RELATIONSHIP BETWEEN APPRENTICE LEADER AND MENTOR

How can we helpfully use those crucibles or defining moment experiences to produce empathy, humility, compassion, and insight? Through the guidance of a mentor, leading the apprentice leader through that time of reflection, the painful lessons need to be learned and fashioned into those character qualities.

THE PRIORITIZATION OF HUMILITY

Arising from the development of the "twice-born" character within the apprentice leader, primarily through the relationship formed with his or her mentor, the primary developmental assessment of that person's leadership gift should focus on whether authentic humility is being developed. The development of humility is of fundamental importance to the subject of leadership. Hastings and Potter contend, "Humility is the first pillar of a leader whom others will trust."[111] This link between humility and trust is an important one. "Twice-born" leaders are those who have not only experienced difficult circumstances but also allowed their character to be formed out of the crucible of those circumstances. Central to what is formed in that crucible is "a deepening sense of self,"[112] which I contend is a crucial aspect of humility. Thus, the "twice-born" leader is in a powerful position to develop humility and therefore the quality of trustworthiness.

The mentor will need to assess the answers to the following questions:

- Is this person open and responsive to criticism?
- Is this person teachable?

- How does this person respond to setbacks and failures?
- How open is this person to change?

THE FORMING OF AN HONEST RELATIONSHIP WITH THOSE THE APPRENTICE WOULD LEAD

As stated above, one benefit of church-based leadership development is the accountability that develops between the apprentice and those he or she will be leading. This accountability needs to be a defined part of the strategy for developing trustworthiness rather than an ad hoc arrangement. Part of the leadership training process involves ongoing practical assignments (the hands aspect of leadership development), such as the leading of small groups, the preparing and facilitating of Bible studies, and being given responsibilities for specific projects, which the mentor and apprentice review. To increase a general environment of trust, however, we should give opportunity for wider participation. Those whom the apprentice has been leading in those practical assignments should be encouraged to give feedback, either verbally or in written form. While feedback always needs to be contextualized and treated with caution,[113] it has the dual benefits of empowering followers and cutting through any false assessments the apprentice has made.

SUMMARY

Therefore, we should not understand the development of a strategy that encourages leader trustworthiness as implying that trust is a leadership tactic to be employed as a tool to elicit a favorable response from followers. Rather, the strategy we have considered here offers structured opportunities for the testing and growth of the character qualities that result in heightened levels of trustworthiness. To summarize, these opportunities involve personal reflection, a developing relationship with a mentor, and the participation of the wider church body—all working together for the purpose of producing mature, spiritual leaders in the church.

The bedrock issue of trust is essential if a leader is to have followers. Followers assess and choose to buy into a leader only after the trust issue is settled; only then do they choose whether to support that leader's vision. Following Sanders, Maxwell correctly points out, "Leadership is influence—nothing more, nothing less."[114] Without the bedrock of trust, leaders cannot influence and therefore will find few willing to follow their cause, no matter how exciting or compelling they are. As Maxwell notes, "You cannot separate the leader from the cause he promotes."[115]

Having considered what causes people to buy into a leader, we now need to examine the cause that leader promotes—the leader's vision.

Section 3

The Need to Regain a Sense of Vision

Chapter 6

Where does vision come from?

THE LEADER'S VISION

ARE LEADERS BY definition visionary people? Writers such as Stanley[116] and Sanders[117] maintain that this is so. For Sanders, "Those who have most powerfully and permanently influenced their generation have been "seers"—people who have seen more and farther than others—persons of faith, for faith (is) vision."[118] We can see this truth worked out in the lives of biblical leaders who were called to leadership on the basis of being granted a vision from God. These leaders include Moses,[119] Nehemiah,[120] and Isaiah.[121] Vision and leadership are inextricably linked. However, many leaders feel deficient in the areas of vision forming and vision casting.

According to a survey conducted among pastors, *Christianity Today* reports the following statistics of those who rated themselves as strong in a given area: only 48 percent in the area of vision casting, 43 percent in the area of building consensus, 42 percent in the area of focusing on goals, and 42 percent in the area of the gift of administration. Creating and implementing a strategy scored 28 percent and 26 percent respectively.[122]

If vision is so important to leadership, clearly we seem to have a problem. But what exactly is the link between vision and leadership? John Maxwell explores this question by asking, "Does the vision make the leader? Or, does the leader make the vision?"[123] For Maxwell, the answer is the former—the vision comes first. As someone begins to perceive and "own" a vision so a leader begins to be born. While vision can exist without leadership to carry it forward, Maxwell doesn't believe that a leader can exist without vision to take responsibility for the people and unite them. I agree with this position; therefore, I contend that a leader is visionary by nature.

Building on this position, we need to understand the source and development of vision in light of the challenges posed by our postmodern culture, which has moved away from a consensus on either the need for, or the viability of, an overarching vision.

The Leader as a Visionary

Where do visions come from? A vision, in fact, can derive from a variety of sources. Blackaby and Blackaby note six potential sources:

- The "Because It's There" Source of Vision.[124] This is a reactionary approach to vision forming, in that the vision is to conquer the obstacle presenting itself without considering the implications or desirability of taking such a course of action. This source of vision takes its name from the answer George Leigh Mallory gave when someone asked him in March 1923 why he wanted to climb Mount Everest.[125]
- The "Duplicating Success" Source of Vision.[126] If a vision has worked elsewhere, either for this particular leader or for others, then some see that vision as being worth repeating. The rise in popularity of the Hollywood movie franchise[127] bears testimony to this as a source of vision.
- The "Vanity" Source of Vision.[128] Desire, often of the leader, for status or adulation drives this type of vision. Nebuchadnezzar is one example of someone who possessed this vision source (Dan. 3:1–7).

- The "Need" Source of Vision.[129] A leader can allow vision to be set through perceived need, an example being the vast amount of money spent on preparing for the Y2K "millennium bug."[130] While perceived need has the obvious advantage of being a popular vision, as Blackaby and Blackaby point out, "a need expressed is not the same thing as a call by God."[131]
- The "Resource Driven" Source of Vision.[132] One can form a vision on the basis that resources are available, resulting in the vision's becoming the expression of the sum total of those resources—a temptation when a company operates a zero-based budgeting system.[133] If one cannot roll over an unspent budget to the following financial year, the temptation is to spend remaining budget dollars before year-end and thus become "resource driven." While vision needs resources, those resources should follow the vision rather than define it.
- The "Leader-Generated" Source of Vision.[134] A vision must come from somewhere, and many would contend that the creation of vision is a leadership function. The leader develops and shares what Collins and Porras call "Big, Hairy, Audacious Goals" (BHAGs).[135] BHAGs can be attractive to church leaders since the concept carries the notion of dreaming big dreams for a big God. However, we must exercise caution in using this concept as a goal. Just because something is "big, hairy, and audacious" does not necessarily mean it emanates from God. Church leaders who adopt the BHAG concept too enthusiastically and uncritically may well lead people toward the achievement of a man-made goal rather than a God-inspired one.

A spiritual leader's vision must emanate from a different source—revelation from the heart of God. The truth is, only God's vision will achieve God's plans, as highlighted in Isaiah 55:8–9, "'My thoughts are nothing like your thoughts,' says the LORD. 'And my ways are far beyond anything you could imagine. For just as the heavens are higher than the earth, so my ways are higher than your ways and my thoughts higher than your thoughts.'"

The leader as visionary is not the author of the vision, but rather the receiver of the vision as a revelation from God. The leader is then the communicator of that vision or revelation to others. Church leader Nelson Searcy writes, "Your vision is defined by your values."[136] This is true in that the vision or revelation God gives the leader will resonate with that leader's God-given core values. However, I believe with Blackaby and Blackaby that if a vision has any source other than God, it is a less-than-authentic revelation. As such, vision will be underpinned by one's values, but not defined by them, emanating as revelation from the heart of God. Values, in turn, will be fed by one's worldview, which should be shaped increasingly by our understanding of who God is and our relationship with Him.

The role of spiritual leaders, therefore, becomes that of interpreting the revelation to those they are leading—inspiring and mobilizing them not only to fulfill that vision but also to find personal fulfillment as a result. The vision's source is of crucial importance since the term *spiritual leader* can encompass a wide array of applications. Discernment Research Group points out that "creative visualization" (the technique of using your imagination to create what you want in life, which has come to be an interchangeable phrase with "visioning" or "vision casting" among many in the evangelical world) is also used in occult settings. "Creative visualization" then becomes the "process of using mental images in order to acquire what one desires or produce changes in one's attitude, thus creating one's own reality."[137] Clearly, creating one's own reality is not the goal of the spiritual leader… the goal here is to discern God's vision and then to lead others into that vision.

Chapter 7
. . . .
The Creative Process of
Growing Vision

THE DEVELOPMENT OF VISION

AS STATED ABOVE, it is my belief that vision comes before the leader. God imparts to the leader the vision, who needs to spend time before God, praying about what this vision might mean. It needs to be formed coherently, and shared with others. Consequently, a healthy leadership culture will have at its heart a process of encouraging potential and emerging leaders to identify that vision or revelation God seeks to impart. This process of receiving and forming the vision will be part of the ongoing discernment of whether that person is, indeed, being given the gift of spiritual leadership. The best forum for this discernment is both formal teaching on the nature and development of vision and ongoing dialogue between mentor and emerging leader. This ongoing dialogue is far more important than many realize.

In Jesus' day, the discipleship process included formal academic learning. Far more than this, however, it involved the imparting of skills, knowledge, morality, and daily godly living from the mentor to the apprentice as the mentor went about his daily routine. Hence the much-repeated blessing directed at disciples of rabbis was "May you be covered in the dust of your rabbi." Literally the dust the rabbi kicked up as he went about his daily routine fell on his disciples as they followed closely behind. Discipleship was more caught than taught. Jesus allowed His disciples to catch His vision, to own it for themselves, and then to lead in the light of it. How is that vision caught, owned, and passed on?

We need to consider five phases in this process.

The Discerning Phase

How is vision first discerned? Hybels refers to this early discernment as "holy discontent,"[138] a sense of discontentment about how a situation currently is, which emanates from God. Nehemiah is an example of someone who experienced this "holy discontent": "They said to me, 'Things are not going well for those who returned to the province of Judah. They are in great trouble and disgrace. The wall of Jerusalem has been torn down, and the gates have been destroyed by fire.' When I heard this, I sat down and wept" (Neh. 1:3–4). Piper maintains that what he calls "holy discontentment" arises from the fact that "leaders are always very goal-oriented people,"[139] as exemplified by the apostle Paul: "…I am still not all I should be, but I am focusing all my energies on this one thing: Forgetting the past and and looking forward to what lies ahead, I strain to reach the end of the race and receive the prize for which God, through Christ Jesus, is calling us up to heaven." (Phil. 3:13–14)

It is important to note that a holy discontentment is not in itself a vision—it precedes and fuels vision. The Teal Trust identifies six stages of developing a vision: preparatory prayer, the gathering together of the "building blocks" (in other words, the past, our experience, what God has already said in prayer, a reflection on the church and community, its needs and pressures), prayer, drafting the vision, and sharing the vision.[140] It is noteworthy that the Teal Trust believes it is preferable for a small leadership group to undertake this whole process rather than a lone leader. One can see the obvious attractions and benefits of this strategy—"Plans go wrong for lack of advice; many advisers bring success" (Prov. 15:22). However, for that group to be effective, each person would need to be fired by the same holy discontent; otherwise division rather than vision could well emerge.

In a healthy leadership culture, mentors encourage leaders-in-training to explore their sense of holy discontent and encourage them to begin translating that into a positive vision of what could be. Tragically in too many local churches, many see this "holy discontent" as evidence of troublemaking, something to be discouraged. In reality, no great vision is born unless one is fueled by a holy discontent. If no structure is in place to recognize this phase and to encourage whoever has discovered a holy discontent rising within him or her to seek positive, godly solutions, more than likely that sense of discontent will degenerate into something negative, or that person will grow increasingly frustrated and disillusioned, eventually leaving the church.

The Developing Phase

If vision is first discerned through the identification of a holy discontent, it is developed through a period of discernment, which involves waiting, praying, and maturing. According to Stanley, "A vision rarely requires immediate action. It always requires patience."[141] The purpose of this waiting period, he maintains, is threefold. The vision must mature within us,[142] we must mature in preparation for the vision,[143] and God is at work behind the scenes, preparing the way.[144] This is an open-ended period of time, during which the emerging leader needs to be working with his or her mentor through this threefold process.

This is also time to authenticate the source and validity of the vision; is it merely a human-sourced BHAG or a genuine vision from God? That authentication process needs to include a number of mature Christians, who form a safe environment. This is not the stage when the vision is cast in its finished form, but rather the stage when the "holy discontent" is assessed by mature Christians to discern whether it originates from the heart of God. These mature Christians are also assessing the potential vision for whether it is a vision for *now*, or for some future time. The mentor's role in this is to take heed of that group's advice and to focus particularly on the character development issues needed to progress that vision.

The Sharing Phase

Once other mature Christians have authenticated this holy discontent and addressed the relevant character issues through the period of discernment, the emerging vision needs to be shared. As Stanley rightly maintains, "All God-ordained visions are shared visions."[145] In analyzing the vision Nehemiah cast, Stanley identifies four components: the problem, the solution, the reason something must be done, and the reason something must be done *now*.[146] A crucial aspect of a healthy leadership environment will be, in my opinion, opportunities for emerging visions to be shared and tested by the wider body, and feedback to be given in a sensitive and constructive manner. As McAllister-Wilson rightly point out,

> The ability of a leader to articulate a bold vision is only half of what it takes to practice a leadership that inspires a *shared* vision. Christianity is a group activity…The *church* is a plural noun, and Christian leadership is like fishing with a net or being a shepherd of a flock; it is about gathering people together and enlisting then in a movement towards a shared vision.[147]

Shared vision, of course, is not the same thing as a leader sharing his or her vision. The latter implies that other people are being invited to endorse the vision of another, which will only at best gain the compliance of those people. A truly shared vision implies a joint ownership of the vision God is challenging His people with, which the leader is articulating. While the leader may well be the first to discern God's revelation, to become a shared vision, it will need to strike a chord with the hopes and dreams of others.

Sharing such a vision needs to occur at several different levels— before a group of peers and one's coach (a grouping I refer to as a "cluster"), before the senior church leadership, and before the church's general wider body. At each stage of this vision-sharing process, feedback should be encouraged. Without welcoming and listening to feedback, no shared vision will occur. Casting the vision effectively requires creative thinking on the part of the vision caster. McAllister challenges vision casters to "learn to tell your story as an epic tale. Practice telling your story as an exciting adventure."[148] Because visions are specific, they need to contain solid plans, but preeminently they need to inspire, to draw people irresistibly into a vivid picture of a better future.

The Implementing Phase

As the Teal Trust point out, "A vision that does not lead to some kind of action is unlikely to be of much help to the church or to God!"[149] Some, however, can enthusiastically endorse the vision in the sharing phase and steadfastly resist it in the implementation phase because the implementation of vision implies change. Finzel points out that "change is driven by vision."[150] However, as Biehl puts it,

> A change can make sense logically, but still lead to anxiety in the psychological dimension. Everyone needs a niche, and when the niche starts to change after we've become comfortable in it, it causes stress and insecurities. So, before introducing change, we have to consider the psychological dimension.[151]

For the implementation of vision to be successful, one must give careful consideration to the effect that vision will have on those niches. Communication is key to implementing vision. Finzel puts it well when he says, "Never assume that anyone knows anything. Communication has to take place over and over and over again. Communication takes place when the person has finally understood (though not, necessarily, agreed with) what you have tried to get across and he or she now repeats what you said back to you and to others."[152] It is a mistake to assume that everyone will enthusiastically embrace the vision once it has been implemented. Rogers's Innovation Adoption Curve, a model that classifies the various rates of adoption of new ideas, shows that just 2.5 percent of people are classified as Innovators; 13.5 percent as

Early Adopters; 34 percent as Early Majority; 34 percent as Late Majority; and 16 percent as Laggards.[153] The Early Majority are defined as "thoughtful people, careful but accepting change more quickly than the average," whereas the Late Majority are described as "skeptic people, [who] will use new ideas or products only when the majority is using it."[154]The Innovation Adoption Curve serves as a reminder that people adopt change at varying rates; therefore, the implementation of vision is a process rather than an event.

The Reviewing Phase

In addition to ongoing communication during the implementation process, regular reviews are also needed. It is a mistake, however, to review the newly-implemented vision too early in its life because a vision needs time to become established. While no prescribed length of time must elapse before a review takes place, it is wise to allow several steps to occur before a review takes place:

- The initial "teething problems" have been identified and worked through.
- At least some early benefits of the newly implemented vision have begun to become apparent.
- The Early Adopters, as defined above, have formed an opinion about the newly implemented vision.

A helpful review will include the following elements:

- A recap of why the vision was implemented. What was life like before this vision?
- An assessment of the benefits that have accrued
- An assessment of the losses that have occurred
- An opportunity for others to speak freely about the physical, emotional, relational, and spiritual impact the newly implemented vision has had on them
- A commitment to refine the vision in light of this review

- A restatement of the mission, the core values, and the core beliefs on which the church is based

MAINTAINING AND REFRESHING VISION

Beyond the initial review of a newly implemented vision lies the maintenance and refreshment of that vision. It is interesting to note that even with a short-term project such as what Nehemiah led the people in Jerusalem to embark on, maintaining and refreshing that vision still needed to occur. Though the building project lasted only fifty-two days (Neh. 6:15), the commitment to the project and the focus on it began to wane part way through the project as other issues arose (Neh. 5:1–5).

How often should a vision be recast? I believe the answer is continually. Nehemiah's experience demonstrates that no matter how effectively and clearly a vision is initially cast and how enthusiastically the people initially embrace it, in a brief time frame the attention and allegiance of followers will wander. Stanley says,

> Regardless of how effectively you cast your vision initially, eventually a team member or two will work out of alignment. He will develop an agenda that is off-center to the vision. Instead of working with the rest of your team, he will be pulling ever so slightly in a different direction. This usually transpires well into the implementation stage of a vision.[155]

Stanley believes that the leader's prime job is to encourage alignment during the vision's life.[156] He sees two forces undermining that alignment: time and "bumps" (or unexpected events, such as crises).[157] What constitutes alignment? Clarity of understanding of the vision, individual passion for the vision, unity of purpose among active participators in the vision, a reassessment of the strategy supporting the vision, and a revision when necessary. As Stanley points out, "Visions are refined—they don't change. Plans are revised—they rarely stay the same."[158] A difference, of course, exists between continually recasting a vision and tinkering with the strategy. The former keeps the vision fresh in the followers' minds, whereas the latter spreads confusion and undermines confidence. While vision needs to be continually recast, we should cautiously approach revising strategy in light of a careful review of the ongoing effectiveness of that strategy.

At Kingfisher, to keep the vision of the church network fresh in people's minds, we hold two "vision evenings" each year. At the January vision evening, we share the leadership team's sense of how the Lord is challenging us over the coming twelve months. In the September vision evening, we review how that sense has translated into reality over the previous nine months. We also communicate what adjustments need to be made to keep that vision on track for the rest of the year.

These are the two major events in the network's life. On their own, they would be insufficient to keep local churches focused on the God-given vision during the year. For that reason, we design a sermon series. We encourage storytelling: testimonies from those who have experienced the outworking of the vision in their lives or who have taken risky steps of faith as a result of responding to the challenges outlined in the vision evenings. We highlight and celebrate every "green shoot of success" each time something happens that is in line with the vision. Over the years we have come to recognize the truth of the saying "Celebrate what you want to replicate!"

It is important to note, however, that fulfilling the vision should never occur at the expense of core values. In this regard Nehemiah's experience is instructive. It is important to note that when calling a public meeting to discuss the various societal issues that had arisen (Neh. 5:7), Nehemiah effectively interrupted the building program. What this act demonstrates is that core values must be upheld over fulfilling the vision at any cost.

If a vision should be continually recast to remain fresh, the question is, "By what means?" A vision is intended to be not merely a lifeless proposition but a living, motivating expression of the people's aspirations and dreams. Consequently, to refresh and recast a vision in the hearts and minds of followers on an ongoing basis, one must be as creative as possible. The vision needs to be recast and refreshed through visual means, such as PowerPoint presentations, graphs and charts, audiovisual presentations, and dramas. It should be recast through stories of individuals and groups who have been affected by the unfolding vision. It should also be recast from time to time by means of verbal presentations—sermons, small-group Bible studies, question-and-answer sessions, and so on.

SUMMARY

Having considered how important vision is, and what it takes to develop vision, it must be said that it is misleading to refer to vision in terms of it being the leader's vision. Though a key aspect of leadership is to discern and develop vision, if followers see the vision as only "the leader's vision," the leader has failed in his or her task to cast that vision. For the leader's vision to achieve its potential, it must become a shared vision incorporating others' hopes and aspirations.

The term "The Leader's Vision" can be misleading for another reason; though the leader is the vision's conduit, the vision did not originate with the leader. The authentic vision has preceded the leader, having originated in God's heart and been entrusted to the leader, initially in the form of a holy discontent. Therefore, within the process of helping potential leaders discern whether God has indeed called them to leadership is the task of enabling them to discern whether they are the carriers of a genuine vision from God. This idea again points to the crucial need for a leadership culture in the local church, where a structure can be developed to enable such development to take place. How might this structure be developed in practice? We now turn to this question.

Section 4

An Example of a Leadership Model

INTRODUCTION

What might a leadership model look like? Adopting the actual model is less important than ensuring that it addresses the issues highlighted in Sections One to Three. Unless the leadership model you adopt is the outworking of the leadership culture in your local church, it will be like using a piece of cloth that hasn't been shrunk to patch an old garment (Matt. 9:16). A leadership model must be more than just another program in an already-too-busy schedule of activities. I have spoken with enough frustrated pastors because their leaders won't attend training events or see the need to develop their leadership gift in other ways to confidently say that a leadership model is only as effective as the culture it comes from. Therefore, if you have decided to skip Sections One to Three in this book, I suggest that you think again!

The leadership model Kingfisher has developed and implemented over the years raises a high bar for those training to be leaders. Stretching over a two-year period, it includes formal teaching, personal reflection, guidance through defining moments with a mentor during personal coaching sessions, practical training, celebration, and three different levels of commissioning. The diagram on page 89 provides an outline of how these pieces fit together. But before we look at the model as a whole, we should consider how we might take the first step in introducing a leadership culture in the local church.

Chapter 8
Moving from Theory to Practice

FIRST STEPS

NOT LONG AGO, I was talking to a pastor about the subject of leadership development. I asked him what approach he had adopted in his church. His reply—which I have heard many times before—was that those performing leadership functions in his church weren't really interested in developing in their roles. They didn't see the need for leadership development; even when training events were conducted, attendance was poor. He had a training budget, but it was rarely used and never used up. Consequently, he couldn't imagine how he could implement a leadership training model. Leaders were appointed on a needs basis, served in the area where they were asked to serve, and led in the way they saw fit. This pastor would have dearly loved to have leaders who were motivated to grow, a structure and strategy for growing and developing new leaders, godly accountability, and an environment where leaders inspired those they led to become fully devoted disciples of Jesus Christ. But where would he start?

That's a very good question. The answer is that the place to start is in the soul of the pastor. It starts with, as Jim Collins puts it, "confronting the brutal facts (yet never lose faith)."[159] This is an essential aspect of the holy discontent we have already examined. To transform the initial nagging sense of unease into a plan of action, we must confront the cold, hard facts. We need to get specific and focus on the gap between what is and what should be. These steps need to be taken in every area of church life, but never more so in the area of leadership. We must have a clear picture of the state of our leadership development as it actually is at this moment and of how leadership development should be. We should not kid ourselves about the gap between the two.

Part of this honest assessment—indeed, the heart of this assessment—is to honestly assess the culture that actually exists in this church. As I have already mentioned, if we downplay the importance of this step or overlook it completely, we are doomed to frustration and failure as we seek to bring in the changes we believe need to be made. What differences currently exist between the current church culture and the leadership culture described in this book? Don't forget: every group of people has a culture, and "culture refers to those elements of a group or organization that are most stable and least malleable."[160] Schein goes on to observe that "the bottom line for leaders is that if they do not become conscious of the cultures in which they are embedded, those cultures will manage them. Cultural understanding is desirable for all of us, but it is essential to leaders if they are to lead."[161]

Spending time assessing the true culture of the church will enable the leader to understand what false assumptions need to be addressed, what fears need to be allayed, and what language needs to be used to paint a compelling picture of the future. Here are some questions to help in this assessment:

- Do people understand the nature of the spiritual gift of leadership?
- Do you need to address bad leadership experiences of the past?
- What is the experience of change in the church? Is it positive, negative, or ambivalent?
- How have you introduced change in the past? Have consultation and vision casting been historically good, or have they merely been announced?

Moving from Theory to Practice

After spending time gaining a clear understanding of the current culture, the vision of a leadership culture needs to be cast among the key leaders in the church. We need to bear in mind when vision casting that it is permissible, even encouraged, for others to express reservations and ask questions. It is important at each step of the way that others feel included in the process and that their views, fears, and suggestions are listened to and taken seriously. As part of this vision-casting process, why not invite your key leaders (if you don't have any key leaders, your "early adopters," those most likely to "get it" when presented with a new idea) to participate in an introductory, one-day leadership course?

As described in the next section, we invite every potential leader to attend a one-day Introduction to Leadership course, which enables a conversation between then, their sponsoring leader, and God about whether they are indeed being called to leadership at this stage. Such a course could be an ideal "appetizer" to begin building momentum among key people in your church, making the implementation of a full-blown leadership model in your church that much easier.

Momentum is the key component of any change introduced in an organization. In this context, the momentum gained by having some leaders participate in a highly motivational one-day leadership course would be valuable indeed. Positive feedback from others is worth a thousand sermons from the pulpit on why this change is necessary. To help you as you consider moving toward this first step, the sessions we cover in our Introduction to Leadership course are as follows:

Session 1—The Spiritual Gift of Leadership

- An analysis of the call to and preparation for leadership through the example of Abraham
- Can the spiritual gift of leadership be removed?
- The life of Christ exemplifies the principles of spiritual leadership.

Session 2—Finding Your Style of Leadership

- Common attitudes all leaders share
- Identifying your particular, dominant style: pioneering, strategic, management, team building, pastoral, or encouraging. (Note: These styles are not mutually exclusive, but it is instructive to come to an understanding of your dominant approach to leadership and to understand the strengths and weaknesses of each style).

Session 3—Learning to Pass the Baton

- Key aspects of apprenticeship as highlighted by Jesus' relationship with His disciples
- Releasing apprentice leaders—the pitfalls and how it can work well

Session 4—Identifying and Avoiding Spiritual Abuse

- The aspects of a spiritually abusive system
- The effects of a spiritually abusive system
- The spiritual gift of leadership and its fruit
- Spiritual abuse of leaders

Session 5—Maintaining a Walk of Holiness

- Some personal aspects of a spiritual leader: integrity, purity, humility, a servant's heart
- Maintaining a walk of integrity and holiness

Session 6—The Prayer Life of a Leader

- The need to develop a regular, powerful, faith-filled prayer life, as exemplified by Jabez in 1 Chronicles 4:9–10

This is just one example of an Introduction to Leadership course. The goal in this context is to build momentum around the vision of establishing a leadership culture in your church. At the end of this one-day course, each participant is awarded a certificate to mark this first step along the journey of leadership development. I cannot overstress the importance of "celebrating the milestones" in church life in general and in leadership development in particular.

A team from Kingfisher recently attended an amazing graduation service at one of the Kingfisher leadership colleges in Malawi. Thirty students had just completed their one-year leadership training course, and we had been invited to speak at the graduation and to present certificates to the graduates. It was a time of incredible joy and celebration as thirty people, who had sacrificed so much to complete the course, were sent out to plant new churches all over southern Malawi. Their relatives had journeyed for days to get to the venue, and it was such a privilege to join with them and witness this great achievement. They had great challenges ahead of them, which made it all the more important that this particular milestone was celebrated. Remember, we need to celebrate what we want to replicate.

THE LEADERSHIP MODEL

Having taken a look in some detail at the Introduction to Leadership course in the context of a first step that could be taken in introducing a leadership culture to the local church, we now turn our attention to one example of a complete leadership model. The overview of the model is as follows:

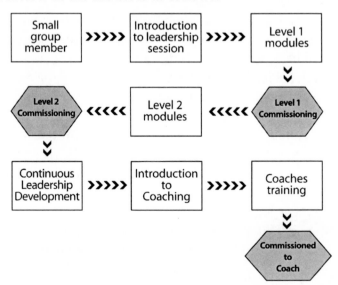

Kingfisher recognizes two broad categories of leadership—ministry leaders and small group leaders. Ministry leaders are responsible for developing church-wide ministries—for example, men's breakfasts, a performing arts ministry for adults with learning disabilities, and so on. The responsibilities of small-group leaders include ministry output, but also include the pastoral oversight and spiritual development of a group of people. The differentiation between these two broad categories enables a more precise approach to training and development since certain skills are more relevant for a potential "small-group leader" than for a "ministry leader" and vice versa.

In addition to these two broad categories, Kingfisher recognizes various levels of leadership, namely, apprentice leader, small-group leader or ministry leader, coach, supervising coach, elder, pastor, and senior pastor. Each level carries different responsibilities and is interconnected in terms of accountability. Small-group leaders, coaches, and supervising coaches all have expectations of fulfilling a mentoring role—thus a coach fulfills both coaching and mentoring responsibilities. While a coach has responsibility for the pastoral oversight and development of a cluster of four or five small-group or ministry leaders, a supervising coach is responsible for the pastoral oversight and development of a similar-sized cluster of coaches.

The leadership model implemented in 2007 has three phases. Level 1 culminates in the recognition of an apprentice leader as having received basic leadership training and thus the commissioning into a church leadership role. Level 2 culminates in the recognition of a leader as having received practical tools for leadership and thus the commissioning. Level 3, the level at which coaches are identified, called, equipped, and released, culminates with the commissioning of new coaches. For leaders to be recognized and authorized, they must be commissioned after having successfully completed several steps. Until leaders are commissioned at level 1, they are regarded as apprentice leaders under the oversight of a commissioned leader. Level 1 encompasses six modules and takes those who are exploring the possibility that they have been given a gift of leadership through an apprenticeship to the point where they are released into recognized leadership.

Introduction to Leadership

As already noted, this one-day course explores the nature of the spiritual gift of leadership, differing styles of leadership, an insight into the process of apprenticeship, and the spiritual disciplines expected in a leader's personal life. This course, which is taught semiannually, is attended by invitation only. Existing church leaders may recognize the potential gift of leadership in someone. In consultation with their coach and by extension the wider church leadership, they may invite that person into the process of discerning whether that gift exists and whether circumstances in that person's life indicate that this is the right time to begin developing that gift.

If after prayer and reflection the person agrees, he or she attends the one-day Introduction to Leadership course. Upon completion of this course, the person attends a feedback session with the sponsor to determine whether it would be appropriate to continue exploring and growing in this leadership gift by entering into Level 1 of the leadership model, which encompasses modules 1 to 6. At this stage, the person, called an "apprentice leader," enters into a formal apprenticeship relationship with the sponsor, who fulfills the role of mentor during the journey through level 1 of the leadership model.

Module 1—School of Theology Level 1

To ensure that Kingfisher leaders possess theological grounding, all apprentice leaders are required to undergo a course called School of Theology. Though the course has two levels, apprentice leaders are only required to successfully complete level one, which encompasses the following six subjects:

- Does God exist?
- Is the Bible accurate?

- Covenant theology
- Messianic prophecies
- The Trinity
- Eschatology

This module is taught in the context of a classroom, incorporating group discussion.

Module 2—Administration Induction

This module deals with practical issues often overlooked in the development of leaders, such as health and safety and general administration. Issues include how to use the photocopier, who to contact if an incident occurs in the building, and so on. The course is in the form of a written document all apprentice leaders must read and understand.

Module 3—Knowledge and Context

This module takes apprentices through the philosophy and structure of leadership at Kingfisher. It consists of a group session on Kingfisher structure and vision and a reading on the following subjects:

- The responsibilities of pastors, elders, and trustees
- The role and purpose of ministries and small groups
- The role and purpose of leaders
- The role and purpose of coaches

Module 4—Leading a Ministry

This module focuses on the general knowledge and understanding needed to lead a successful ministry. Each of the five sessions in this module offers a teaching element recorded on CD, which apprentices will listen to in their own time. Each session provides an opportunity for personal reflection and response, which apprentices will discuss with their relevant mentors. The topics in this module include the following:

- Community building
- Developing and carrying vision and strategy
- Developing the spiritual gifts of those you are leading
- Confidentiality
- The prayer life of a leader

Modules 5 and 6 are specifically designed for those training to be small-group leaders. Successful completion of these two modules include practical application within group settings, incorporating feedback and reflection with their mentor and where appropriate with the group involved in the practical application.

Module 5—Small-Group Leader Training (1)

This module, taught in a classroom session with practical application in a group setting and feedback, covers the following topics:

- Group dynamics
- Running a small group
- Leading a Bible study (how to prepare and deliver)

Module 6—Small-Group Leader Training (2)

Following on from Module 5, this module is also taught in a classroom setting with practical application in a group setting and feedback. Using both formal teaching and role-playing, it covers the following:

- The boundaries between pastoral care and counseling
- Effective facilitation skills

Mentors meet regularly with apprentices to encourage reflection and personal growth, helping them through issues raised and challenging them to grow and develop in every aspect of their spiritual lives. The twin aspects of mentoring and coaching are intertwined since a rigid separation of the two would be artificial and unhelpful.

Level 1 of the leadership model typically takes a year to complete. During that time, the apprentice leaders receive many opportunities to practically apply all they are learning and are encouraged on a journey of personal reflection and feedback.

When all modules have been successfully completed and both the mentor and the apprentice are satisfied that sufficient character development has complemented the knowledge gained, the mentor recommends to the coach, who in turn recommends to the elders and pastors, that the apprentice be commissioned as a leader. This commissioning takes place at the annual leadership conference when the apprentice is commissioned into a specific area of ministry. Whether commissioned to be a small-group leader or a ministry leader, the apprentice is placed in a cluster of other small group leaders and ministry leaders under the oversight of a coach. The coach meets each leader in his or her cluster every month to offer personal support and encourage spiritual growth as well as to direct each person to grow and develop in the spiritual gift of leadership. Every two months, all leaders at Kingfisher attend a celebration event. This is an opportunity for all leaders to worship the Lord together, to pray together, to be updated on any news they need to share with their group or area of ministry, and to feel connected to the big picture of where the church as a whole is headed.

The second phase of the leadership model—Level 2—aims to equip leaders and provide practical tools for ongoing leadership growth. Consisting of five modules, this phase takes a newly-commissioned leader and imparts the tools necessary for effective small-group or ministry leadership.

Module 7—Community

Taught in a classroom setting, this module examines the following:

- Understanding community
- The dynamics of understanding and managing change
- Becoming an effective agent of change

- Understanding and applying the communications triangle, which charts different levels of communication that affect the level where the group currently is and that encourages or discourages progress up the triangle toward more meaningful communication.

This module includes group work within clusters, facilitated by the coaches, in order to reflect on the leader's personal understanding and application of community, confidentiality, and change.

Module 8—Personal Discipleship

The aim of this module is to come to a greater understanding of how God has created each of us. Out of this module, leaders begin to develop a Spiritual Pathways Growth Plan. Alongside the spiritual health plan all small group members at Kingfisher are encouraged to develop, this will help the leaders grow more effectively in the ways God has made them. Specifically, this module covers the following:

- What are spiritual pathways?
- Becoming more effective through understanding how God made each of us
- What is a Spiritual Pathways Growth Plan, and how will it help develop leaders in their spiritual journeys?

The second part of this module takes place in the setting of a personal coaching session with the leader's coach. The leaders reflect on their personal discipleship and on the implications of using the growth plan in their group or area of ministry.

Module 9—School of Theology Level 2

Continuing the desire expressed in module 1—School of Theology Level 1—to ensure a theological grounding for all leaders, this module focuses on five subjects, spread over seven sessions, and encourages participants to form a reasoned, biblically-based opinion of each. The seven subjects are the following:

- The case for creation
- The case for a historical flood
- The case for the accuracy of Bible prophecy
- The case for God's plan of salvation revealed in the Feasts of Israel (three sessions)
- The case for the resurrection

The approach of the School of Theology Level 2 is not to push one specific "party line" so much as to encourage participants to become confident in investigating these issues and arguing for the outcome they feel to be the most reasonable.

Module 10—Discipling Individuals

This module is presented in two parts. The first part is a taught session, and the second part is completed via 1-2-1 with a coach. Pre-reading is provided for the taught part of this module on the following topics:

- An explanation of Rohnke's comfort, stretch, panic model
- Understanding how to motivate others

The taught part of this module encompasses two major topics:

- What is a fully-devoted follower of Jesus Christ?
- Bandwidth—what it is and how we can practically use it

Module 11—Apprenticing, Incorporating an Appreciation of Emotional Intelligence

This module builds on the apprenticing session in the Introduction to Leadership course and introduces emotional intelligence. Topics include the following:

- How do you spot a potential apprentice?
- What is emotional intelligence?
- How can we use the insights of emotional intelligence? (In particular, how can we use the core competencies of self-awareness, self-management, social awareness, and relationship management in the development of apprentices and ourselves?)

Introduction to Coaching

The coach's role is crucial to the development of a leadership model. A coach acts in a role that is not too dissimilar to that of a church pastor, carrying significant responsibility for the growth and spiritual well-being of a large number of people. At Kingfisher, a coach has spiritual oversight of and responsibility for about forty people. They are expected to develop several small group or ministry leaders so that those leaders can lead effectively. In this big task, finding those who can successfully fulfill this role isn't easy. One mistake is to appoint a coach too quickly; spiritual maturity and emotional maturity are essential characteristics for this role. Leaders must have demonstrated that maturity by how they have reflected on and dealt with their defining moments. They must have consistently demonstrated emotional intelligence in the way they have handled themselves under pressure and created resonance among other leaders. When leaders consistently display these traits and demonstrate the ability to think and plan at a strategic level, the church senior leadership may invite them to consider becoming a coach.

Recognizing the significant expectations placed on coaches at Kingfisher, we have specifically designed this module to enable leaders to discern whether a coaching role is right for them. Using both classroom elements and role-playing, this module teaches the following:

- A definition of the term *coach*
- Comparing and contrasting coaching and mentoring: when is one more appropriate than the other?

- The expectations of a coach—both what is expected of a coach and what a coach can expect in terms of support and ongoing training
- Some practical coaching tools, such as the TGROW (Topic, Goal, Reality, Options, Way forward) model, what questions a coach should ask, and what development strategies a coach should help a leader put in place
- How to help leaders develop through their defining moments

As with the Introduction to Leadership course right at the start of the leadership model, this Introduction to Coaching course is designed to enable someone considering a potential call to coaching and the senior church leadership to come to a mutual understanding of whether God is indeed calling that person to a coaching role at this time. Consequently, a feedback session—or potentially several sessions—needs to take place in which prayerful reflection is encouraged. If the outcome determines that a coaching role is right for that person at this time, he or she should become an apprentice coach and embark on the third level of the leadership model—Coaches' Training.

Coaches' Training

Coaches have four opportunities to meet together each year. These meetings are a mixture of training and mutual support, led by the staff member responsible for leadership development. The following basic coaching skills need to be learned:

- Managing expectations—both what leaders expect of a coach and what a coach should expect of a leader
- How to create positive challenges for people to encourage them to move on in their leadership development
- Facilitation skills and conflict resolution

While coaches teach and discuss these subjects during their training sessions, the primary emphasis is placed on encouragement and the support of apprentice and commissioned coaches.

When Is a Coach Commissioned?

All commissioning takes place as part of the annual leadership conference, which is a one-day gathering of all leaders and apprentice leaders in the Kingfisher Network. Apprentice coaches are deemed ready to be commissioned when they have completed the coaching skills mentioned above and have consistently displayed maturity of character and spiritual walk in their roles as apprentice coaches.

Continuing Leadership Development

Though the leadership model has a beginning and an end, a leader should remain a lifelong learner. Just as disciples of Jesus Christ can never say they have learned all there is to learn about following Him, so leaders can never say they have learned everything to do with leadership. All of us are still learning! My constant prayer almost every day and for the past twenty years of ministry is "Lord, please make me a better leader!" In fact, I'm more aware of my shortcomings in this area now than I was twenty years ago. I'm more mindful of my character deficiencies, my desire to avoid conflict, and the ability I have to fudge issues rather than to confront them when they need to be. We can't measure our growth as leaders based on whether leadership is becoming easier. We can only really see our growth as leaders based on the size of the leadership responsibilities God has entrusted to us (Luke 19:11–27). The more He entrusts us with, the more we need to grow as leaders. Consequently, ongoing training is needed. At Kingfisher, we call this training Continuous Leadership Development. Our Continuous Leadership Development program takes the form of two half-day sessions per year. The topics for those sessions are determined according to what the coaches and senior leadership discern that the Holy Spirit has called us to tackle at that time. Topics have included the following:

- Understanding and managing change
- The art of giving and receiving feedback
- Managing our physical, mental, emotional, and spiritual energy
- Leadership pitfalls and how to avoid them
- Communication skills

The Continuous Leadership Development program is open-ended and should be tailored to meet the needs of your particular local church situation. The goal of this program is to encourage your church leaders to continue growing in the spiritual gift of leadership and to continue regarding themselves as learners. When leaders cease to be learners, they move into maintenance mode, and the leadership culture ceases to be an environment where people are growing together and disciples are being developed and grown. We are called to be pioneers, not settlers. By definition, pioneers have not yet arrived; they are still moving forward, still growing, still learning. Twenty years have passed since I attended theological college, but I am more aware today of how far I still need to go and how much I need to grow as a leader. My constant prayer over the past twenty years has been "Lord, make me a better leader!" This should be the prayer a leadership culture encourages in the local church.

Conclusion

MANY HAVE OFTEN claimed that the Chinese symbol for crisis is, in fact, two symbols, one overlaying the other—danger and opportunity. Whether this is true or not, it points to an important truth—that the crisis the local church faces in the twenty-first century presents an incredible opportunity. The crisis of leadership is on our hands. The danger is that an already-marginalized church will become increasingly irrelevant in a society where, according to a 2007 Tear Fund survey, only 10 percent of the population in the UK attend church regularly.[162]

The opportunity presented to us is that declining church attendance and the lack of leadership in society, which the church should provide, could cause us to say, "Enough is enough!" This could well be the church's opportunity to wake up and realize society's desperate need to find a spiritual and moral pathway leading to life—and that the church is God's agency on earth to provide that leadership. As the writer of Proverbs so wisely notes, "Without wise leadership, a nation falls; there is safety in having many advisers" (Prov. 11:14). Wise leadership is in short supply. The stage is set for the church to take her God-ordained place in society once more!

But how can the church lead society when it cannot lead itself? Leadership is not merely an optional specialization of the church; it is God's ordained role for the church in society, and the place to start is by developing wise leadership within the church. However, leaders are not grown by accident. Although leadership is a spiritual gift, it needs a particular environment to flourish and develop just like every other spiritual gift. In such an atmosphere, disciples of Christ find encouragement to grow, using whatever gifts God has given them. Some specifics of the atmosphere created by a healthy leadership culture are as follows:

- People have confidence that they can be open and vulnerable without being judged, condemned, or made to feel that they are somehow letting their side down.
- People are encouraged to discover and operate in their spiritual gifts. With this atmosphere comes a desire to release people into their God-given areas of ministry, rather than to coerce them into the jobs that need to be done.
- Within godly accountability, many experience true freedom. Freedom is not about the absence of boundaries as the Prodigal Son discovered (Luke 15:11–24), but about godly accountability that encourages spiritual growth and maturity. An interplay between teaching, challenge, and free will provides guidelines, gives right incentive, and allows freedom of choice.
- New converts are taught about Jesus Christ rather than indoctrinated into the rules of the organization. They learn to be members of the kingdom before they learn to be members of the church. They become enthusiastic about Jesus rather than loyally supportive of the leadership.
- The people respect, honor, and submit to leadership, but not out of fear, through coercion, or because of a belief that God will reward them. Godly leaders are honored, respected, and submitted to because that is the response they evoke from others. Honor, respect, and submission are the natural responses to a supernatural anointing. If they need to be

insisted upon, then the spiritual gift of leadership is absent, and the emergence of an unhealthy system is likely.

Who would not want to be part of that kind of church? Who would not want to be led by emotionally intelligent, called, anointed, equipped, supported, and accountable leaders? My passion is for the church to become all God has called it to be, to become "the shaper" of society, rather than "the shaped" by society. Paul said to the church in Rome, "If God has given you leadership ability, take the responsibility seriously" (Rom. 12:8). That truth is generally understood on an individual basis, but it is equally relevant, perhaps even more so, when applied to the local church as a whole. God has given the local church a leadership role and a leadership ability; it's up to us to take those seriously. Leadership is much more than merely requiring the world to change or to become like us. That is not the message of the incarnation. The incarnation is about God becoming like us.

"Though he was God, he did not demand and cling to his rights as God. He made himself nothing; he took the humble position of a slave and appeared in human form. And in human form he obediently humbled himself even further by dying a criminal's death on a cross" (Phil. 2:6–8). True leadership comes when the church becomes incarnational—not demanding and clinging to our rights as children of God, but connecting with those we are seeking to share the Good News with. It includes entering into the world of those who are lost and hurting and earning the right to show them that there is another, better way.

At Kingfisher, many are single parents, and many are divorced. Many are struggling with addictions and have criminal records. The Lord doesn't desire these believers to experience any of these trials, and we certainly haven't lowered the bar as far as encouraging people to live holy, God-honoring lives. To be an incarnational church, however, means that we will be reaching and connecting with real people living in the real world. It takes "twice-born" people to really connect with "twice-born" people.

Likewise, we need "twice-born" leaders who possess the credibility and moral authority to provide leadership to a "twice-born" world. The church all too easily discounts people who have a past, especially when considering others for leadership positions. But what if we turned that problem on its head and saw past mistakes, when properly understood and worked through, as being the very things God could use to raise up "leaders with chests"? Perhaps these people have recognized and grown through past experiences, been helped through their defining moments, and become more emotionally intelligent as a result.

I truly don't believe that the church is no longer relevant. On the contrary, I believe that under God the church is the hope of the world. The world at its worst desperately needs the church at its best. A world that has lost its way and its confidence in the wake of terrorist attacks, the credit crunch, a global recession, and failed promises from politicians desperately needs anointed, credible, trustworthy leadership. As Banks and Ledbetter put it, "An interest in leadership…tends to appear during periods of widespread uncertainty and rapid change."[163] We are living in those times. Now is the time for the church to step up and answer that call.

Bibliography

Anderson, Neil T. *Victory Over the Darkness*. Jackson, Miss:Monarch Books, 2000.

Banks, Robert, and Bernice M. Ledbetter. *Reviewing Leadership: A Christian Evaluation of Current Approaches*. Grand Rapids: Baker Academic, 2004.

Bennis, Warren, and Robert Townsend. *Reinventing Leadership: Strategies to Empower the Organization*. London: Judy Piatkus Publishers Ltd., 1995.

Blackaby, Henry T., and Richard Blackaby. *Spiritual Leadership: Moving People on to God*. Nashville: Broadman and Holman Publishers, 2001.

Bosch, David Jacobus. *Transforming Mission: Paradigm Shifts in Theology of Mission*. New York: Orbis Books, 1991.

Burn, James. *Fishing for the King*. Chichester: New Wine Press, 1997.

Burns, James MacGregor. *Transforming Leadership*. London:Atlantic Books, 2003.

Cannistraci, David. *Apostles and the Emerging Apostolic Movement*. Ventura, CA: Renew Books, 1996.

Cloud, Henry, and John Townsend. *How People Grow*. Grand Rapids, MI: Zondervan, 2001.

Collins, Jim. *Good to Great: Why Some Companies Make the Leap...
and Others Don't*. London:Random House, 2001.

Collins Jim, and Jerry I. Porras. *Built to Last: Successful Habits of
Visionary Companies*. New York: HarperCollins, 1997.

Collinson, Sylvia Wilkey. *Making Disciples: The Significance
of Jesus' Educational Methods for Today's Church*. Milton
Keynes:Paternoster, 2004.

Covey, Stephen R. *Principle-Centered Leadership*. New York:Simon
and Schuster, 1992.

Csorba, Les T. *Trust: The One Thing That Makes or Breaks a Leader*.
Nashville: Thomas Nelson, 2004.

Edmiston, John. *Biblical EQ: A Christian Handbook for Emotional
Transformation*. Charleston:BookSurge Publishing, 2008..

Finzel, Hans. *Change Is Like a Slinky*. Chicago: Northfield
Publishing, 2004.

Forman, Rowland, Jeff Jones, and Bruce Miller. *The Leadership
Baton*. Grand Rapids, MI: Zondervan, 2004.

Frost, Michael, and Alan Hirsch. *The Shaping of Things to Come:
Innovation and Mission for the 21st-Century Church*. Peabody,
MA: Hendrikson Publishers, 2005.

George, Carl F., and Warren Bird. *How to Break Growth Barriers:
Capturing Overlooked Opportunities for Church Growth*. Grand
Rapids, MI: Baker, 1993.

Goleman, Daniel. *Emotional Intelligence: Why It Can Matter More
Than IQ*. London: Bloomsbury Publishing, 1996.

Goleman, Daniel, Richard E. Boyatzis, and Annie McKee. *The
New Leaders: Transforming the Art of Leadership*. London: Time
Warner Books, 2003.

Harvard Business Review on Leadership. Boston: Harvard Business
School Press, 1998.

Harvard Business Review on the Mind of a Leader. Boston: Harvard
Business School Press, 2005.

Hastings, Wayne, and Ronald Potter. *Trust Me: Developing a
Leadership Style People Will Follow*. Colorado Springs, CO:
WaterBrook Press, 2004.

Bibliography

Hybels, Bill. *Courageous Leadership*. Grand Rapids, MI: Zondervan, 2002.

Hybels, Bill. *Holy Discontent: Fueling the Fire That Ignites Personal Vision*. Grand Rapids, MI: Zondervan, 2007.

Hybels, Lynne, and Bill Hybels. *Rediscovering Church: The Story and Vision of Willow Creek Community Church*. Grand Rapids, MI: Zondervan, 1995.

Johnson, David, and Jeff VanVonderen. *The Subtle Power of Spiritual Abuse: Recognizing and Escaping Spiritual Manipulation and False Spiritual Authority Within the Church*. Minneapolis: Bethany House, 1991.

Johnston, Graham. *Preaching to a Postmodern World: A Guide to Reaching Twenty-First Century Listeners*. Leicester: InterVarsity Press, 2001.

Kimball, Dan. *The Emerging Church: Vintage Christianity for New Generations*. Grand Rapids, MI: Zondervan, 2003.

Kouzes, James, and Barry Z. Posner B. *A Leader's Legacy*. San Fransisco, CA: Jossey-Bass, 2006.

Kouzes, James M., and Barry Z. Posner. *Credibility: How Leaders Gain and Lose It, Why People Demand It*. San Francisco: Jossey-Bass, 2003.

Kouzes, James M., and Barry Z. Posner, eds. *Christian Reflections on the Leadership Challenge*. San Francisco: Jossey-Bass, 2004.

Lewis, C. S. *The Abolition of Man*. New York:Macmillan, 1947.

Marshall, Thomas. *Understanding Leadership*. St. Ives: Sovereign World Ltd., 1991.

Matthews, Gerald, Moshe Zeidner, and Richard D. Roberts. *Emotional Intelligence: Science and Myth*. Cambridge, MA: The MIT Press, 2002.

Maxwell, John C. *Developing the Leader Within You*. Nashville: Thomas Nelson, 1993.

Maxwell, John C. *The 21 Indispensable Qualities of a Leader: Becoming the Person Others Will Want to Follow*. Nashville: Thomas Nelson, 1999.

Maxwell, John C. *The 21 Irrefutable Laws of Leadership: Follow Them and People Will Follow You.* Nashville: Thomas Nelson, 1998, 1999.

McAlpine, Rob. *Post Charismatic?* Eastbourne: Kingsway Communications Ltd., 2008.

Murray, Stuart. *Post-Christendom: Church and Mission in a Strange New World.* Milton Keynes: Paternoster Press, 2004.

O'Neill, Onora. *A Question of Trust: The BBC Reith Lectures 2002.* New York:Cambridge University Press, 2002.

Ortberg, John. *God Is Closer Than You Think.* Grand Rapids, MI: Zondervan, 2005.

Rainer, Thom S. *Breakout Churches: Discover How to Make the Leap.* Grand Rapids, MI: Zondervan, 2005.

Reynolds, Larry. *The Trust Effect: Creating the High Trust, High Performance Organization.* London: Nicholas Brealey Publishing, 1998.

Sanders, J. Oswald. *Spiritual Leadership: Principles of Leadership for Every Believer.* Chicago: Moody Press, 1994.

Schein, Edgar H. *Organizational Culture and Leadership.* San Francisco: Jossey-Bass, 2004.

Stanley, Andy. *Visioneering: God's Blueprint for Developing and Maintaining Vision.* Sisters, OR: Multnomah, 1999.

Viola, Frank. *Who Is Your Covering? A Fresh look at Leadership, Authority, and Accountability.* Present Testimony Ministries, http://www.ptmin.org, 2001.

Endnotes

1. Burns, *Transforming Leadership*, 2.
2. "Tony Blair: Mention God and you're a 'nutter,'" *Daily Telegraph* Web site, http://www.telegraph.co.uk/news/main.jhtml?xml=/news/2007/11/25/nblair125.xml (accessed November 2007).
3. Murray, *Post-Christendom*, 19.
4. Kouzes and Possner, *Credibility*, xiii.
5. David Watson was a leading evangelical in the UK in the 1970s and 1980s. Ordained as an Anglican Vicar, Watson was prominent in the Charismatic Renewal movement until his death, from cancer, in 1984.
6. Forman, Jones, and Miller, *The Leadership Baton*, 23.
7. Ibid., 24.
8. Ibid., 25.
9. John Kotter, "What Leaders Really Do" in *Harvard Business Review on Leadership* (Boston: Harvard Business School Press, 1998), 53.
10. Kimball, *The Emerging Church*, 233.
11. Hybels, *Rediscovering Church*, 193.
12. Schein, *Organizational Culture and Leadership*, 17.
13. Ibid., 395.
14. Forman, Jones, and Miller, *The Leadership Baton*, 102.

15. Ibid., 103.
16. Goleman, Boyatzis, and McKee, *The New Leaders*, 67.
17. Fred Smith, "Spotting a New Leader," *Leadership* 17 (Fall 1996): 4:31-33, quoted in Forman, Jones, and Miller, *The Leadership Baton*, 103.
18. Ortberg, *God Is Closer Than You Think*, 121.
19. Kotter, "What Leaders," 51.
20. Anderson, *Victory Over the Darkness*, 52.
21. Ibid., 66-67.
22. Ibid., 68.
23. Forman, Jones, and Miller, *The Leadership Baton*, 65-69.
24. Cloud and Townsend, *How People Grow*, 122.
25. Ibid., 134-135.
26. Forman, Jones, and Miller, *The Leadership Baton*, 100.
27. Ibid., 100.
28. Blackaby and Blackaby, *Spiritual Leadership*, 20.
29. Max DePree, quoted at http://www.nwlink.com/~donclark/leader/leadqot.html (accessed July 15, 2009).
30. Matthews, Zeidner, and Roberts, *Emotional Intelligence*, 10.
31. "Emotional WHAT?" 6 Seconds Web site, http://jobfunctions.bnet.com/abstract.aspx?docid=94380), (accessed July 2009).
32. D. Goleman, "What Makes a Leader?" in *Harvard Business Review on the Mind of a Leader*, 101–102.
33. Goleman, *Emotional Intelligence*, 103.
34. Daniel Goleman, "Emotional Intelligence of Leaders," *Leader to Leader* (Fall 1998), 22, quoted in Hybels, *Courageous Leadership*, 184.
35. Goleman, Boyatzis, and McKee, *The New Leaders*, 6.
36. Goleman, "What Makes," 102.
37. ECI-360, the Emotional and Social Competency Indicator 360. This is a 360 degree tool to assess the emotional and social competences of individuals in organizations.
38. Emotional Quotient Inventory (EQi) test assesses five broad sub-types of emotional intelligence: intrapersonal intelligence,

interpersonal intelligence, adaptability, stress management, and general mood.

39. Multifactor Emotional Intelligence Scale (MEIS) was later developed and revised to form Mayer, Salovey, and Caruso Emotional Intelligence Test (MSCEIT).

40. Matthews, Zeidner, and Roberts, *Emotional Intelligence*, 518.

41. Edmiston, *Biblical EQ*, 5.

42. Goleman, Boyatzis, and McKee, *The New Leaders*, 6.

43. Ibid., 67.

44. Ibid., 67.

45. Zaleznik, Abraham "Managers and Leaders—Are They different?" in *Harvard Business Review on the Mind of a Leader*, 75.

46. Zaleznik, "Managers and Leaders," 88.

47. Blackaby and Blackaby, *Spiritual Leadership*, 37

48. Ibid., 10.

49. Ibid., 29.

50. Rainer, *Breakout Churches*, 42.

51. Sanders, *Spiritual Leadership*, 18.

52. Forman, Jones, and Miller, *The Leadership Baton*, 146.

53. Ibid., 25.

54. Hugh. Mackay, *Why Don't People Listen?* (Sydney: Pan Macmillan, 1994), 14–15, quoted in Johnston, *Preaching to a Postmodern World*, 64.

55. Mind Tools Web site, http://www.mindtools.com (accessed September 2007).

56. Mind Tools Web site, http://www.mindtools.com/CommSkll/CommunicationIntro.htm (accessed September 2007).

57. Words in brackets are mine.

58. Rainer, *Breakout Churches*, 42.

59. Kotter, "What Leaders," 41.

60. Rainer, *Breakout Churches*, 43.

61. "coach and mentor definitions," The Coaching & Mentoring Network Web site, http://www.coachingnetwork.org.uk/ResourceCentre/WhatAreCoachingAndMentoring.htm (accessed November 2007).

62. Kotter, "What Leaders," 41.

63. Blackaby and Blackaby, *Spiritual Leadership*, 20.
64. Stanley, *Visioneering*, 179.
65. "Authority and Accountability in the Leadership Culture of a Local Church."
66. Tacitus, quoted in Maxwell, *The 21 Indispensable Qualities of a Leader*, 41.
67. "Kingfisher Church—INFORMATION," Kingfisher Church Web site, http://www.kingfisher.org.uk/information/beliefs.html (accessed November 2007).
68. Burn, *Fishing for the King*, 43–44.
69. George and Bird, *How to Break Growth Barriers*, 19.
70. Ibid., 19.
71. Johnson and VanVonderen, *The Subtle Power of Spiritual Abuse*, 20.
72. Ibid., 32.
73. Ronald E. Enroth, *Churches That Abuse* (Grand Rapids, MI: Zondervan, 1993), quoted at http:www.apologeticsindex.org/a04.html (accessed July 15, 2009).
74. *New Bible Dictionary*, Second Edition, (Leicester: InterVarsity Press, 1982), 108.
75. Menno Simons, quoted in Marshall, *Understanding Leadership*, 111.
76 Frost and Hirsch, *The Shaping of Things to Come*, 170.
77. Ibid., xi.
78. Synan, Vinson. quoted in Cannistraci, *Apostles and the Emerging Apostolic Movement*, 77.
79. Ibid., 55.
80. Ibid., 29.
81. Frost and Hirsch, *Things to Come*, 172, footnote 11.
82. ,Viola, Frank, *Who Is Your Covering?* (Present Testimony Ministry, 2001), quoted by McApline, Rob, *Post-Charismatic?*, (Eastbourne:David C.Cook Kingsway Communications Ltd, 2008), 201.
83. McAlpine, *Post Charismatic?*, 157.
84. Derek Prince, Bob Mumford, Don Basham, Charles Simpson and Ern Baxter. Originally Prince, Mumford, and Basham

birthed the Holy Spirit teaching ministry out of a desire to bring spiritual depth to the growing charismatic movement in the 1960s.

85. McAlpine, *Post Charismatic?*, 191.
86. Kimball, *Emerging Church*, 45.
87. Bennis and Townsend, *Reinventing Leadership*, 63.
88. Nancy Ortberg, *Christian Reflections on the Leadership Challenge*, 90.
89. Csorba, *Trust*, 3.
90. Reynolds, *The Trust Effect*, 5.
91. "Irish Catholic Church Rapidly Losing Influence," National Secular Society Web site, http://www.secularism.org.uk/irishcatholicchurchrapidlylosing.html (accessed October 2007).
92. Humphrey Taylor, "Who Do We Trust the Most to Tell the Truth?", Harris Interactive Web site, http://www.harrisinteractive.com/harris_poll/index.asp?PID=145 (accessed October 2007).
93. Institute of Business Ethics Web site, http://www.ibe.org.uk/Briefing_4_Surveys07.pdf (accessed October 2007).
94. Bennis and Townsend, *Reinventing*, 61f.
95. Csorba, *Trust*, 63.
96. Reynolds, *Trust Effect*, 9.
97. Ibid., 10.
98. Ibid., 25.
99. Reynolds, *Trust Effect*, 9
100. Ibid., 9
101. Johnston, *Preaching to a Postmodern World*, 69.
102. Ibid., 72.
103. Bosch, *Transforming Mission*, 361.
104. Ibid., 360
105. Ibid., 360
106. Csorba, *Trust*, xxiii.
107. Ibid., xxiii.
108. Ibid., 64.
109. Lewis, *The Abolition of Man*, 34–35.

110. Cloud and Townsend, *How People Grow*, 207.
111. Hastings and Potter, *Trust Me*, 15.
112. James Heskett, "Are Business Schools really Important 'Crucibles' of Leadership?", *Working Knowledge from Harvard Business School*, 2001, quoted in Csorba, *Trust*, 223.
113. Issues such as personal agenda, the life circumstances of the person giving the feedback, and the potential resistance to being asked to give feedback at all need to be taken into consideration when assessing given comments.
114 Maxwell, *The 21 Irrefutable Laws of Leadership*, 17.
115. Ibid., 147.
116. "Visions are born in the soul of the man or woman who is consumed with the tension between what is and what could be," Stanley, *Visioneering*, 17.
117. "Leadership is influence," Sanders, *Spiritual Leadership*, 26.
118. Ibid., 55.
119. Exod. 3. God grants Moses a vision of his people being led out of captivity into the Promised Land.
120. Neh. 1. Nehemiah is moved by the plight of Jerusalem, out of which comes an implied vision for the rebuilding of the city.
121. Isa. 6: 1–8. Isaiah is commissioned through the medium of a vision from God.
122. John C LaRue, Jr, "Qualities of Pastoral Leadership", *Christianity Today* Web site, http://www.christianitytoday.com/yc/2004/003/15.72.html (accessed December 2008).
123. Maxwell, *Developing the Leader Within You*, 140.
124. Blackaby and Blackaby, *Spiritual Leadership*, 57.
125. Elizabeth Knowles, "A Quote from George Leigh Mallory," Ask Oxford Web site, http://www.askoxford.com/worldofwords/quotations/quotefrom/mallory/ (accessed March 2008).
126. Blackaby and Blackaby, *Spiritual Leadership*, 58.
127. An example is the *Rocky* movie franchise distributed by Metro-Goldwyn-Mayer.
128. Blackaby and Blackaby, *Spiritual Leadership*, 60.
129. Ibid., 60.

Endnotes

130. "The Millenium Bug Crisis," BBC Web site, http://www.bbc.co.uk/dna/h2g2/A191521 (accessed March 2008).
131. Blackaby and Blackaby, *Spiritual Leadership*, 61
132. Ibid., 63
133. "Zero-Based Budgeting," Reference for Business Web site, http://www.referenceforbusiness.com/management/Tr-Z/Zero-Based-Budgeting.html (accessed March 2008).
134. Blackaby and Blackaby, *Spiritual Leadership*, 65.
135. Collins and Porras, *Built to Last*, 93.
136. Nelson. Searcy, Smart Leadership Web site, http://www.smartleadership.com/magazine/view.asp?id=27 (accessed June 2007).
137. John Lash, *The Seeker's Handbook* (New York, Harmony Books, 1990) quoted in "Rick Warren & Vision Casting," Discernment Research Group Web site, http://www.herescope.blogspot.com/2005/10/rick-warren-vision-casting.html (accessed June 2007).
138. Hybels, *Holy Discontent*, 25.
139. John Piper, "The Marks of a Spiritual Leader," Desiring God Web site, http://www.desiringgod.org/ResourceLibrary/Articles/ByDate/1995/1575_The_Marks_of_a_Spiritual_Leader/ (accessed July 2007).
140. The Teal Trust Web site, http://www.teal.org.uk/vl/vl4proc.htm (accessed July 2007).
141. Stanley, *Visioneering*, 20.
142. Ibid., 20.
143. Ibid., 21.
144. Ibid., 24.
145. Ibid., 85.
146. Ibid., 86.
147. David McAllister-Wilson, *Christian Reflections*, 59.
148. Ibid., 59.
149. The Teal Trust Web site, http://www.teal.org.uk/vl/vl4proc.htm (accessed October 2007).
150. Finzel, *Change Is Like a Slinky*, 84.

151 Bobb Biehl, *Increasing Your Leadership Confidence* (Sisters, OR: Questar Publishers, 1989), quoted in Maxwell, *Developing*, 52.

152. Finzel, *Slinky*, 200.

153. "Innovation adoption curve of Rogers," Value Based Management Web site, http://www.valuebasedmanagement. net/methods_rogers_innovation_adoption_curve.html (accessed October 2007).

154. Ibid.

155. Stanley, *Visioneering*, 165–166.

156. Ibid., 166.

157. Ibid., 166.

158. Ibid., 158.

159. Collins, *Good to Great*, 65.

160. Schein, *Organizational Culture*, 11.

161. Ibid., 23.

162. " 'One in 10' attends church weekly", The BBC website, http:// news.bbc.co.uk/1/hi/uk/6520463.stm (accessed October 2008).

163. Banks and Ledbetter, *Reviewing Leadership*, 21.

Lightning Source UK Ltd.
Milton Keynes UK
26 February 2010

150662UK00002B/2/P